COMING INTO

THE WEALTHY PLACE

A secret path to abundance few will ever discover.

DAVE WILLIAMS

COMING INTO THE WEALTHY PLACE

A secret path to abundance few will ever discover.

Unless otherwise noted, Scripture quotations are taken from the King James Version of the Bible.

Scripture quotations noted TLB are from *The Living Bible*, Copyright ©1971. Used by permission of Tyndale House Publishers, Inc., Wheaton, Illinois 60189. All rights reserved.

Scripture quotations noted NLT are from the *New Living Translation*, Copyright ©1996. Used by permission of Tyndale House Publishers, Inc., Wheaton, Illinois 60189. All rights reserved.

ISBN 0-938020-76-5

First Printing 2004

Cover By: Robison Gamble Creative

Published by

DECAPOLIS PUBLISHING

Printed in the United States of America

BOOKS BY DAVE WILLIAMS

15 Big Causes of Failure

36 Minutes with the Pastor

7 Sign Posts on the Road to Spiritual Maturity

ABCs of Success and Happiness

Angels: They Are Watching You!

Art of Pacesetting Leadership

Cave of Depression

Christian Job Hunters Handbook

Deception, Delusion, & Destruction

Developing the Spirit of a Conqueror

End Times Bible Prophecy

Faith Goals

Filled: With the Mightiest Power in the Universe.

Genuine Prosperity

Getting to Know Your Heavenly Father

Gifts that Shape Your Life & Change Your World

Grand Finale

Grief and Mourning

Growing Up in Our Father's Family

Heard from the Lord Lately?

How to be High Performance Believer

Lonely in the Midst of a Crowd

Miracle Results of Fasting

New Life...The Start of Something Wonderful

New Life-Spanish

Patient Determination

OTHER BOOKS BY DAVE WILLIAMS

Questions I Have Answered
Radical Fasting
Radical Healing
Radical Forgiveness
Regaining Your Spiritual Momentum
Revival Power of Music
Road to Radical Riches
Secret of Power With God
Slain in the Spirit
Somebody Out There Needs You
Success 101
Supernatural Gifts of the Holy Spirit
Supernatural Soul Winning
The AIDS Plague
The Beauty of Holiness
The Desires of Your Heart
The Jezebel Spirit
The Pastor's Minute
The Presence of God
The World Beyond
Tongues & Interpretation
Understanding Spiritual Gifts
What to Do if You Miss the Rapture
Your Pastor: A Key to Your Personal Wealth

CONTENTS

*Jesus paid the price
for our salvation, which includes
our healing and our deliverance
from poverty and lack.*

INTRODUCTION

If you have ever been to a large hotel, you know that some people stay on the first floor, some on the second floor, and so on. The higher you go the more the rooms cost because they have better views and more amenities. And if you want a room on the top level, the concierge level, you need a special elevator key.

Many Christians have never spent a night on the concierge level, so they don't know what it's like. I've been there and I can tell you: it is wonderful! You have someone ready to serve you at all times. If you need something ironed, you call the concierge and he or she gets it pressed for you. If you need tickets to a play or concert, the concierge books the tickets. There are refrigerators stocked with food, racks of videos, magazines, books and CDs. The view from the window is always terrific. It's a luxurious place where most people dream of staying only once or twice in a lifetime — maybe on a special anniversary.

But many people never make it to the concierge level even once.

This book is about living on the concierge level of life, which I call *The Wealthy Place*. It is about releasing the power to get wealth. Many people reading this book — perhaps you — are positioned to move into the ministry of wealth. We are going to talk about that throughout these pages.

But there are conditions to reaching *The Wealthy Place,* and not everyone will meet them. You see, Jesus promised that he who is faithful over little will be trusted with much.

> His lord said unto him, Well done, thou good and faithful servant: thou hast been faithful over a few things, I will make thee ruler over many things: enter thou into the joy of thy lord.
>
> —Matthew 25:21

The Wealthy Place isn't about prioritizing money. It is about putting God's interests first! It's about pursuing His purposes in these last days. And when we do that, God heaps blessings on us as we go. Deuteronomy 28, starting in verse 2, says that when we hearken unto the Lord, He will cause *thirty different blessings to chase us.* We will be lenders, not borrowers, the head and not the tail. We will live on the concierge level, not the first floor or stuck in some corner near the noisy hotel pool.

If you follow the principles I share with you in this book, you will enter into The Wealthy Place.

If you follow the principles I share with you in this book you will enter into *The Wealthy Place.* You will enjoy the power of genuine prosperity. Jesus paid the price for our salvation, which includes our healing and our deliverance from poverty and lack. Many Christians live as if they don't know that. But we are approaching a time when we will need people who have received the ministry of wealth to fulfill God's purpose for the Church before Christ's return.

I want to teach you the exciting, life-changing principles that have already propelled many to *The Wealthy Place*. Will you listen…and move up to the concierge level?

Dave Williams

Lansing, Michigan

M*oney doesn't go to people who need it. It goes to those who manage it properly for the King.*

CHAPTER 1

CHASING RAINBOWS

Twenty some years ago Guy Richardson, a member of our church, graduated from Oral Roberts University and had no idea what he was going to do with his life. He began applying God's principles of wealth, and in a recent year his business achieved $43 million in gross sales.

Another young man didn't have much going for him when he started out 10 years ago. He wasn't properly educated, yet he put into motion God's radical wealth principles, and last year his tithe (10% of his income) was more than $50,000.

Some people find *The Wealthy Place*, but many more never do. They live on level one, two, or even three, and they think that is as good as it gets. But those first levels are just the beginning. There is much more for us, brother or sister! Christians should be moving up to higher and higher levels of wealth and responsibility, managing the resources God has put into this earth as the men in my examples have done.

I no longer understand why anyone is content with little. A typical married man works one or more jobs, and his wife also works. They have a house in suburban America and two cars. He thinks he's happy! He thinks he is prospering, but he's not; he is in poverty because he's spending his life chasing dollars instead of having dollars chase him. He's on the first floor working himself to death, knowing nothing about life on the concierge level. He has to work two jobs, and his wife has to work just to keep up their so-called "middle class" life-style. The kids don't know their parents, and the family never knows true wealth. They live in a form of poverty!

It's painfully clear that people don't know how to handle money unless they are taught.

When I talk about *The Wealthy Place*, I'm talking about the outrageous wealth God is willing to pour into His people. The more revelation God gives me about money, the more radical and determined I get! You and every other Christian should insist on moving up to the top floor and having money chase you instead of the other way around. I have been on the first floor, the concierge level, and everything in between, and I'm convinced that *The Wealthy Place* is where Christians belong.

PIPE DREAMS

In the introduction of my top-selling book, *Radical Riches,* I told the story of when I was eight years old. It was close to the fourth of July, and I wanted to find the pot of gold at the end of the rainbow. I wanted some money to buy firecrackers — Roman candles, ladyfingers, M-80s, silver salutes, cherry bombs you name it. One day my friends and I disobeyed our parents and followed a rainbow for six miles but never found that pot of gold. We were disappointed, deflated, and our pockets were as empty as when we began.

That's a picture of the life many people choose to lead. They chase rainbows, thinking they're going to find a pot of gold. They go after lotteries, casinos, good-luck charms, and get-rich-quick schemes.

I pastor a church with more than 4,000 members, and 70 percent of the prayer requests I get every week pertain to financial problems. You wouldn't believe what people write.

"Pray that I will be able to refinance my house so I can pay off my credit cards."

"Pray that the bank will approve our new home equity line of credit."

Wealth and knowledge are not found in rainbows, lotteries, casinos, or good luck.

"Pray that I will get financing for my new car."

"Pray that I will have enough income so I can start tithing."

I sometimes want to stamp a big "STUPID" on the card and send it back to the person who submitted it. Then I remember, I too was in the same place for many years of my life!

It's painfully clear that people don't know how to handle money unless they are taught. God said:

> My people are destroyed for lack of knowledge...
>
> —Hosea 4:6a

Wealth and knowledge are not found in rainbows, lotteries, casinos, or good luck. They are not even found in prayer requests that ask God to bless the mismanagement of money.

A man came to our office not long ago and asked for $300 from our Help Fund. An associate minister sat with him and listened as the man explained that his $270 paycheck had been stolen. He was asking for $300 because he said the Lord wanted to bless him. The minister asked how he had lost the money, and he said a prostitute stole it from him while he was witnessing to her. The minister asked how it happened, and he said, "I was in a room witnessing to a prostitute, and another prostitute in the room next door took the money out of my pants." This guy was caught with his pants down! He had handled money and morality poorly and lost what he had. We didn't give him any money.

We've all done stupid things before (though maybe not *that* stupid). I'm sure you can point to money mistakes in your own past. I sure can.

I was with my family in the Bahamas once, and we went to the beautiful Atlantis Hotel where you can walk through the plexiglass tunnels and see sharks swimming around you. There are amazing beaches and pools, but to get to them you have to walk through a monstrous casino. Early one day my family was walking through the casino to get to the pools, and nobody else was around. The other guests, I suppose, had spent the night gambling and drinking, so they were sleeping in.

The amount of wealth we enjoy in this life will be according to our management of the wealth God entrusts to us now.

I had always wanted to try a slot machine, but I didn't want my mom (who was vacationing with us) to know. And I certainly didn't want my wife or kids to know either. So I took my time and hung back until they were out of sight, then I ducked down and put a quarter in the slot machine. I pulled the handle, the wheels clicked into place, and the machine started ringing and flashing. Money poured out, "Plunk, plunk, plunk, plunk, plunk!" The sound of the coins hitting the steel tray was almost deafening. Everyone turned around and looked at me. I saw my mother, hands on her hips, and my wife Mary Jo rolling her eyes. My kids were both laughing. I was humiliated. It was fun for a moment, but that's not the door to *The Wealthy Place!* I could pull slots all of my life and never get another return, and I would slide deeper into financial hell.

Oh yes…I repented. I felt awful about what I had done and the poor example I had set.

THE POWER TO GET WEALTH

The Bible gives all kinds of signs directing us to *The Wealthy Place*. Deuteronomy 8:18 says:

> But thou shalt remember the LORD thy God: for it is he that giveth thee power to get wealth, that he may establish his covenant which he swear unto thy fathers, as it is this day.

God is not careless in what He says. He means every word. He said plainly, He has given you and me the power to get wealth. Ephesians 3:20 confirms this:

> Unto him, who is able to do exceedingly abundant above all that we could ask or think according to the power that worketh in us.

God has given His children the power — not the skill or talent, necessarily, but the *power* — to get wealth, and the amount of wealth we enjoy in this life will be according to our management of the wealth He entrusts to us right now.

Jesus told a parable in Matthew 25 about a master who gave three of his servants some talents. He wasn't talking about the talent to play the trumpet, or preach, or sing. *He was talking about money.* He gave one man five talents, another man two talents, and another man one talent. You might as well say he gave $5,000, $2,000 and $1,000. It ultimately belonged to their master. They were like junior investors working with the firm's money.

It is critical to understand that nothing we have belongs to us; we are just managers. We are managing what God has entrusted to us. If you become greedy or think it all revolves around you, you will find yourself leaving the concierge level and going down to the lower floors on that elevator, and maybe even into the musty-smelling basement.

The man with $5,000 invested it and turned it into $10,000. The man with $2,000 also doubled his investment and made $4,000. But the $1,000 manager had a different attitude. Doomed by fear, he decided to play it safe. He buried the money so it would be "safe," in his backyard. The master came back to find out what they had done with his money. To the first two, he said, "Well done you good and faithful servants. You've been faithful over a little, now I'm going to give you charge over much." They had managed the money well and passed the test. They didn't fall into the traps many Christians today fall into, where money leaks out and disappears because of poor decisions. Because of their wise management, he took them up to the concierge level.

Then he came to the one who had buried the money. This one made excuses as people with a poverty, first-floor mentality always do. He said, "I knew you were a hard taskmaster, reaping where you don't sow and sowing where you don't reap. Here's the $1,000 you gave me." The master responded, "You lazy and wicked servant! You did not multiply the money I entrusted to you, therefore, I am taking it from you and I'm giving it to the other guys." (I've paraphrased this whole exchange; see Matthew 25 for the story.)

This strikes many of us as unfair. The other guys didn't need it, right? Right. But this is a law of the Kingdom: *Money doesn't go to people who need it. It goes to those who manage it properly for the King.*

You MUST understand that. This principle is so important to your wealth that I'll expound on it more in the next chapter.

E*ach individual bears
the responsibility for either
planning or not planning
for wealth.*

CHAPTER 2

HOW CHRISTIANS MISMANAGE WEALTH

Often Christians get on their knees and say, "God, I need $1,000; send it to me, just send it to me." And they want it to drop out of the sky like rain. They hear stories of unmarked envelopes full of cash showing up in mailboxes. That does happen occasionally, but in all of my life I have never seen a single dollar "rain" out of the sky.

Have you ever dug a hole in your backyard and found a treasure chest full of $100 bills? Does a cash envelope show up every month to cover your bills? Of course not, because that is not how God's system works.

Each individual bears the responsibility for either planning or not planning for his or her wealth for discovering or not discovering the principles that lead to *The Wealthy Place*. Many Christians don't realize that God put the power in us to *create and enjoy wealth.*

Proverbs 10:22 says:

> The blessing of the LORD, it maketh rich, and he addeth no sorrow with it.

In other words, it should be fun for Christians to obtain wealth! There's not going to be sorrow, overwork, and alienation from family. No gimmicks or precarious schemes. Just sound management with a proper amount of faith risk.

Nobody ever gets to The Wealthy Place without planning for it.

My opinion is that Christians ought to operate the major television networks, grocery stores, and banks. It has always appalled me that a church should have to crawl to a bank and beg for money. I fully expect that someday, as the ministry of wealth grows within the Church, banks will come to the Church to borrow money! I'm looking forward to the day when bankers can't find the money to loan to the housing developers, so they come to the Church to try to borrow from us. We will get to say, "Let me check your records here. Fill out this form and that form." The Bible says:

> For the LORD thy God blesseth thee, as he promised thee: and thou shalt lend unto many nations, but thou shalt not borrow; and thou shalt reign over many nations, but they shall not reign over thee.
>
> —Deuteronomy 15:6

Do You See Yourself Wealthy Or Poor?

In 1983 one out of every 425 Americans was a millionaire. By 2004, one out of every 125 Americans was a millionaire. There are more millionaires today than ever before. It is fully attainable for every Christian on the planet to be one of them. Don't you think God wants us to control at least some of the wealth for His glory? Why else would He give His people the power to get wealth?

Nobody ever gets to *The Wealthy Place* without planning for it. How about you? Have you planned to be wealthy? Or have you limited your vision and stuck yourself on the first or second floor of life? For fourteen years I lived in the ghetto, but I became rich in the second half of those years. You see, I learned to be rich on the inside before I was rich on the outside. Life eventually caught up with the vision I had.

The Bible talks so much about money and wealth, prosperity, abundance, and overflow that we can't afford to overlook it if we hope to be all God has called and created us to be. I mentioned Ephesians 3:20 which says, "Now unto him that is able to do exceeding abundantly above all that we ask or think, according to the power that worketh in us." One version adds two more big words: "dream or imagine."

Have you ever sat back in your chair during your prayer time and imagined the wealth God is able to bring to your family or your home? Have you spent time dreaming about what it would be like to have thousands of dollars each month to spend, give and invest? Have you stopped to dream and imagine what you could do for the Kingdom of God? For the poor? For your family? The vacations you could take, the car you could drive, and the home in which you could live? Have you ever really bothered to imagine? If not, you may be out of synch with what the Bible teaches us about wealth.

What if someone gave you $1,000 a day to spend? What would you buy or invest in? Do you have it all figured out yet? If you don't, you probably don't have a plan for your wealth. You probably haven't dreamed and imagined what it would be like to have a few million dollars. You would have to spend $1,000 a day for two years and nine months to spend a million dollars! That's $30,000 a month more than a lot of people earn in a year. Yet it's easily attainable if you will come into *The Wealthy Place* by following the simple principles I am going to give you. I didn't say they were *easy*; I said they are *simple*. They take work and self-control, but they can be understood in a matter of minutes.

People not living in *The Wealthy Place* are always pursuing money. People who live in *The Wealthy Place* are not chasing money; they are attracting wealth!

Later in this book, I will give you a principle that only a handful of people on planet Earth will ever discover and put into practice. It is so powerful it can bring you unimaginable wealth in a short time if you are willing and obedient. I'm going to give you a simple plan for coming out from where you are and entering into a wealthy place. It doesn't matter where you start. You can arrive at the concierge level!

HARD CASH

Let's get one thing straight: When I talk about *The Wealthy Place*, I'm talking about money, not spiritual wealth. I mean cash, gold, silver, real estate, hard assets. Spiritual wealth, of course, is paramount. But the purpose of this book is to talk about physical, tangible wealth the kind that can build church facilities, print Bibles, give grants to children's ministries and scholarships to church planters and Bible school students.

There are many things more important than money, but money is important. If it wasn't, God wouldn't have talked about it so much.

- You can't send your children to the best schools without money.

- You can't have church facilities without money.

- You can't operate lights or have a sound system without money.

You have to be rich on the inside before you can be truly rich on the outside.

- You can't drive to work without money to put gas in the car.

Money is important! It is fully consistent with the Bible for you to have incredible amounts of wealth and still be a friend of God. In fact, you can do a lot of good things when you think in terms of wealth instead of poverty — when you think like a millionaire instead of a person barely eeking out a living.

THINKING WEALTHY

One time I tried to calculate what my time was worth. I calculated how much money I had raised for ministry business through letters, how much money I've raised by writing books and developing strategic relationships. I figured out that my time is actually worth $4,000 an hour. Knowing that changed the way I made decisions. A wealthy person knows that if he has to wait two hours in an airport, that's $8,000 just to get a $270 ticket. Would it make better sense to have his own plane? Probably. But people who don't think in terms of wealth never figure out what their time is really worth, and so they muddle through life, wasting time and money. Then they turn around and criticize those who do think in terms of wealth.

The Queen of Sheba saw Solomon's massive prosperity and abundance, and her breath was taken away. She declared God was the true God and decided to invest in Solomon. She gave him over $80 million in gold, not counting the spices and everything else she brought with her. And Solomon was already a multibillionaire. I supposed she wanted to plant some money — faith seeds — into a life that could bring her the same kind of harvest as Solomon enjoyed.

Have you ever thought what it would be like to have $80 million? What would you do with it? You might say, "That was Solomon. That's not for me." But the new covenant did not erase the blessings of the old one!

You were meant to be like Solomon! How do I know this? In Matthew 6:29-30, Jesus said:

> And yet I say unto you, That even Solomon in all his glory was not arrayed like one of these. Wherefore, if God so clothe the grass of the field, which to day is, and to morrow is cast into the oven, shall he not much more clothe you, O ye of little faith?

Why do people worry? Because they don't have money. Only when you don't have money do you worry about what to wear, where to live, what to drive, and how to fix the water heater and the roof.

> **But seek ye first the kingdom of God, and his righteous-
> ness and all these things shall be added unto you.**
>
> —Matthew 6:33

What is Jesus saying? Seek first (as a priority) to do things God's way. It's that simple. Then...all the things other people worry about getting will be added unto you. No fret. No worry.

What "things" is Jesus talking about? The same things Solomon had! But it's not by direct pursuit. You don't get wealthy by going after $80 million. Rather, *as you go after the things of God, the $80 million comes after you!*

Don't pursue wealth. Let wealth pursue you by prioritizing your life using God's priorities.

This may sound like hocus pocus, but it's not. And it's not just theory. I've lived this way for many years now. I believed in prosperity when I was broke. I knew there was a wealthy place, a concierge level. It shouldn't be a secret to anyone, so I'm going to show you clearly what is robbing God's people of getting up to the concierge level. It's subtler than you think.

In my experience, I've found that almost 96 percent of people fall for a trap and lose the key to the concierge level. You could actually be a millionaire overnight. For example, the children of Israel were in bondage one day, and the next, they were incredibly wealthy. It happened in one day with the favor of the Lord. Think what could happen in just twenty years if we would place God's priorities at the top of our daily lists.

If you simply obey the Scriptures, in twenty years, certainly you can become at least a millionaire. I don't care what your annual salary is. I don't care how much money you currently earn or where you work. You can do it.

So put your mind on living at the concierge level, enjoying the view and the clean air up there. On the top floor you can see more than anyone else; you can relax. It's where you belong, and *you have within you the power to get there!*

Next we'll examine the foundational practices that lead to *The Wealthy Place.*

*G*od wants you to
control the wealth because
He knows what you will
do with it.

CHAPTER 3

AN ANOINTING FOR WEALTH

A few years ago, something very powerful happened to me. I received an anointing from God for radical wealth. In 1998 a well-known, established prophet, Dick Mills, secretly prophesied over me in the parking lot of a restaurant in Lansing, Michigan. He said that in two years God was going to pour upon me an anointing for wealth. I wrote it down in my prayer journal and over the months forgot about it.

Exactly two years later in October, a fresh anointing came upon me. God began giving me revelation about wealth and His purposes for it. I could barely contain myself. I lost all sense of time.

I sat at my computer, writing the revelation as fast as I could. I would write for twelve, thirteen, and even fourteen hours at a time, thinking that only a few minutes had passed.

I remember thinking, "Well, I had better go to dinner," and looking at the clock, to my amazement, it was four o'clock in the morning. I thought it was only six o'clock in the evening.

These revelations became a book called *Radical Riches*. At that time suddenly money started coming to me, and not just to my ministry but to me personally. It was almost as if God was saying, "I can trust you now."

One day the phone rang and it was another fellow Christian who said, "I have a word for you from the Bible. God is giving you an anointing for wealth." This person gave me a Scripture from the Book of Psalms about oil being poured over Aaron's head and running down his beard and robe to his feet.

> It is like the precious ointment upon the head, that ran down upon the beard, even Aaron's beard: that went down to the skirts of his garments.
>
> —Psalm 133:2

This friend said, "You're going to have this anointing for radical wealth, and it will run down onto those who listen and apply these principles and sit under this anointing. They, too, are going to come into an anointing of radical wealth."

Strange and supernatural things started happening to me when that anointing hit me. Here's just one example. A young man sent me a letter. He graduated from Bible school, launched into full-time ministry, and was now serving as a traveling evangelist. He said God told him to give me $10,000, which he planned to do over the course of a year. He was just starting out with a new family and I tried to discourage him from doing it, but he insisted. A $1,000 check came in the mail. Then a $700 check and then a $300 check, then $2,000 — all made out to me personally. This was a new experience to me. At the end of the year, a $6,000 check came. He'd planted $10,000 into my life! Why? *He said he did it to obey God and to plant a seed in the kind of anointing that he wanted on his life.*

Right after that, he e-mailed me and said he had just bought two new properties. Then he bought a few more. Now he's become a major landlord and has all kinds of wealth flowing into his life. I saw him pull into the church parking lot the other day in a Corvette. Understand me: God doesn't

Plant a "seed" into the kind of anointing YOU want.

care what you drive. This young man could afford to buy the car he wanted. Not only is his ministry skyrocketing, speaking in churches all over, he told me that within just a few short months after planting that "seed," his own personal net assets grew by over $100,000.

Countless other wealth-related things began happening.

THE PRIMARY PURPOSE OF WEALTH

Mary Jo and I learned over the years to manage and invest our money wisely. We made some incredibly good investments, and God blessed us. Our wealth didn't come because our paycheck increased, and that's one of the things we'll learn about *The Wealthy Place* you don't get there by having a larger income. We'll discuss that later.

Suddenly, as money began chasing us, we had more money than we needed to live. We're pretty simple people. We don't have extravagant tastes. We live in a little three-bedroom house in a nice neighborhood with the woods behind us. We drive used cars. We try not to buy things we don't really need, but one time I bought a couple of condos in Florida because I felt that God was telling me to. Their value doubled in just one year, so I had more wealth. I have become a so-called "money magnet." I sometimes get criticized over this, nonetheless what I touch usually turns to gold. I don't know exactly how it happens, but I believe it's because God can trust me with wealth, and I've learned how to manage it in a way that pleases Him.

Wealth doesn't come from an increased paycheck.

Here's the first thing I want you to understand about wealth and the resources of the earth: God intends them to be used for the furtherance of the Gospel, the benefit of the Kingdom, and the establishment of His covenant in the earth. That's His overriding purpose for prospering His children.

Before I ever had wealth, Mary Jo and I made the Kingdom of God our top financial priority. We established a charitable foundation, Strategic Global Mission. We started it with $230,000, and some years later turned it into a 501(c)3 and raised public support as the law requires.

People contributed to our foundation, although at first Mary Jo and I were the principal givers. We gave scholarships to Bible college students in South Africa. Today each one is in full-time ministry changing the fabric of that country. They had a reunion recently, and I sent them a letter that was read publicly. They all went wild. They appreciate me. They even name their kids after me. A bunch of "Davids" are running around South Africa and elsewhere because I directed my money toward Kingdom purposes!

Before I owned the island condos or had good investments working for me, I learned this basic principle: God gives us wealth primarily for the Gospel and to establish His covenant. I'll lose some people here because they only want to hear how to enrich themselves, but that's okay. You, dear reader, will stick with me and become a stellar money manager and you will find yourself living on the concierge level of life.

BUILD THE RIGHT HOUSE

In Haggai, chapter one, we learn that people were buying luxurious homes and trying to live in *The Wealthy Place*, but their lives were breaking down. They were planting many seeds but getting little harvest. They tried to get ahead but were frustrated. They had slipped out of *The Wealthy Place* and were heading to lower floors on a runaway elevator.

> Ye have sown much, and bring in little; ye eat, but ye have not enough; ye drink, but ye are not filled with drink; ye clothe you, but there is none warm; and he

that earneth wages earneth wages to put it into a bag
with holes.
—Haggai 1:6

It would be like getting a paycheck, but things are falling
apart in your luxurious house and you can't keep up with the
expenses. They couldn't figure out what the problem was, so
God told them point blank. He said through the prophet
Haggai:

Because of mine house that is waste, and ye run every
man unto his own house.
—Haggai 1:9b

In other words, they put *their* stuff before God's stuff! Big
problem.

You may wonder why you're frustrated, why you're not
getting a harvest. Perhaps you're putting your own house
before God's house, or your own interests before God's interests.

I lived in a little two-bedroom bungalow in a poor neighborhood for fourteen years because the church I pastored was
building a 3,000-seat sanctuary, and I felt it wasn't right for
me to buy myself a house when God's house was still being
built. I built His house first before I bought my new house.

Why didn't I move somewhere else, even though I could
have? For one thing, God didn't tell me to move. I wasn't
going to move for the sake of moving just because my house
was in a neighborhood with drug houses and drunks everywhere. I conducted their funerals when they died. I'd visit
them when they had strokes and couldn't move. And you

know what? A lot of them met Jesus because I lived in that neighborhood.

One ol' drunk prayed the sinner's prayer with me at least fifteen times. It wouldn't make any difference in his life. The next day he'd come by saying, "D-a-a-v-e, you got some coffee? Can you run me to the store to buy some milk?" I quit running him to the store to buy milk because the "milk" was always in a little paper bag with a skinny neck! But one day he showed up at church and genuinely gave his life to Jesus, and that time it stuck.

Then there was Helen, 80-something years old, and she accepted Jesus. Her husband Maynard had a stroke, and we went over to witness to them. My daughter drew a picture of Jesus hanging on the cross and pasted it on the wall where Maynard had to see it all day. She asked if he wanted to accept Jesus, and tears ran down his face. He nodded the best he could, and prayed the prayer of salvation. He took off for Heaven, and I did his funeral.

Why didn't I leave that ghetto-like neighborhood? Because God told me to stay there. *His Kingdom purpose always comes first.* I could have afforded to get out of there years before I did, but I stayed because I chose to obey God.

HAGGAI'S EXPERIENCE

Wealth is a matter of putting God first in everything.

> But seek ye first the kingdom of God, and his righteousness; and all these things shall be added unto you.
>
> —Matthew 6:33

When the children of Israel began to worship God in earnest and build His house, something happened. Here's the principle. It always works this way: *When we do what God says first, then a little way down the road, we're going to get everything He promises.*

> For thus saith the LORD of hosts; Yet once, it is a little while, and I will shake the heavens, and the earth, and the sea, and the dry land; And I will shake all nations, and the desire of all nations shall come: and I will fill this house with glory, saith the LORD of hosts.
>
> —Haggai 2:6-7

Something marvelous and magnificent always follows the glory. When we seek God's glory, it's a universal principle that we'll get something later on. Recall that Solomon didn't ask for riches, but for wisdom so he could lead the nation in a proper way. God said because Solomon asked for wisdom, He'd also give him the wealth to go along with it.

Back to Haggai. So, the glory came in, and then God said:

> The silver is mine, and the gold is mine, saith the LORD of hosts. The glory of this latter house shall be greater than of the former, saith the LORD of hosts: and in this place will I give peace, saith the LORD of hosts.
>
> —Haggai 2:8-9

If you want gold, you want silver, and you want the wealth seek God's glory!

Can He trust you?

> ...and the wealth of the sinner is laid up for the just.
>
> —Proverbs 13:22

The "just" are those who are justified by faith because they have accepted Jesus Christ. Some well-meaning but misinformed Christians say this refers only to spiritual wealth. But what kind of spiritual wealth does a sinner have? None!

The psalmist was once envious of the financial prosperity of the wicked, and then he went into the sanctuary and God gave him this secret: "The end of them is coming. I'm letting them get wealth because there is coming a day when it'll transfer over to the just." After that divine revelation he was no longer envious of the sinners' wealth.

If you want gold, you want silver, and you want the wealth — seek God's glory!

Are you one of those whom God can trust with money? God wants you to control the wealth because He knows what you will do with it. The Bible says the righteous advance the cause of good.

I heard about one wealthy man in another part of the world who spent millions flying his Boeing 747, with full entourage, to other countries visiting fast-food restaurants whenever he wanted a Big Mac or a taco. You and I wouldn't do that. Someone with Kingdom priorities would invest the money to send construction crews to the mission field to build more churches.

Do you see that the concierge level is open to you? Are you starting to formulate a plan for getting there? Next we'll see how to take that first step toward *The Wealthy Place.*

*Living in the
"mediocre room" breeds
stinginess, fear, and greed.*

CHAPTER 4

GETTING OUT OF THE MEDIOCRE ROOM

You've got a choice when you hear about *The Wealthy Place*: you can receive it, or you can reject it. One time when I was preaching on this subject, I had a supernatural revelation that some people in the sanctuary had deliberately not brought money to the service because they were afraid there was going to be a special offering appeal. They were afraid God would tell them to give their money away.

That's a sign you're living in a lower level of financial blessing. It shows disobedience and an improper management of God's resources. It shows the mindset of someone who is not living in *The Wealthy Place* but in a place of mediocrity and lack.

Let's Imagine...

Picture it this way. You live in a room that's boring and bland. It's the room of mundane and mediocre living. Your needs are met, and they always will be, in this mediocre room. You get up, go to work, get your paycheck, make your house payment or pay your rent, make your car payment, your stereo payment, and your furniture payment. You scrape up enough to put in the church offering when the offering plate goes by. If you don't have enough money that week, you take a dollar bill and fold it up into a little square so nobody knows it's only a dollar. Then you go back home to "The Mediocre Room." It's not a fun place to be.

Right next door to you is an opulent, luxurious room called "*The Wealthy Place.*" You peek under the door and see how full and luxurious it is. Soft, soothing music plays, and it's a hundred times more spacious than the room in which you abide. It's a place of peace and plenty.

You try the door handle, but it's locked and you have no idea how to open it. You spend hours wondering how to move from your mediocre room into the opulent room next door. You think, "If only I could get into that wealthy place, I'd have it made." Sometimes you stick your finger under the door or fashion a coat hanger to bring over some of the stacks of money you see sitting there. Now and then you snag a dollar or maybe five out of *The Wealthy Place*, but that door is locked. The wealth and luxury never fully come into your room.

Living in that mediocre room breeds stinginess, fear and greed. It leads people to reject God's true principles of wealth. *It's the opposite of the way God wants you to live!* He does not want

ANY of His children to live in "The Mediocre Room," and yet most do. Why? Let's find out.

LITTLE TENANTS

Let's say you buy a rundown apartment building with 24 units and 24 cranky tenants. One day you decide to recondition and upgrade the whole building. You raise the rent a little. But instead of cheering the progress, the tenants are unhappy. They don't want the rent raised. It's as if they enjoy the old crispy wallpaper peeling off the walls. They gripe and fight and cause you grief until they either move out or come to accept your plan.

Those tenants are like the thoughts living in your mind — thoughts learned from childhood onward. "Money doesn't grow on trees." "We can't afford it." "If you want money, you have to work hard and get a job with good benefits." These and other false beliefs are tenants buried in our minds. They start arguing when you talk about coming into *The Wealthy Place*. These thoughts, like little tenants, gripe, complain, and criticize. They develop all kinds of excuses for *not* coming into *The Wealthy Place*. They create mental conflict within you.

One of the tenants says, "The secret of wealth is to get a second job." Another says, "Work harder and get more overtime." Another says, "Join the union and picket for more pay." Another says, "Get into a business and start selling phone cards or some other product." In spite of all these "tenants'" suggestions and opinions, you always find yourself in the same mediocre, mundane room. It may be dressed up a bit, but it's

You must know the secret: You have the key to The Wealthy Place.

certainly not *The Wealthy Place*. Why? You work so hard, yet still can't seem to get into the room of luxury, wealth, and riches!

What is the key? You must know the secret. These mental tenants do not know the mystery of wealth. The secret is, you've had the key to *The Wealthy Place* all along. It's like the magician locked in the jail. He had a little piece of metal and said he'd be out within 10 minutes. Thirty minutes later he was still trying to pick that lock and couldn't get out. He was so frustrated that he leaned against the door, and it flung open. It had never been locked in the first place.

REJECT OR RESPOND?

God has given you the key to *The Wealthy Place*. It's found in His Word. Jesus paid for your sins; He purchased your salvation, your healing, and your deliverance from poverty. He has given you the key to *The Wealthy Place* — the concierge level of life — but, like the jailed magician, most people don't know it. Later on, I'm going to give you the single principle that will change your financial life forever, the one that draws all these other principles together. But first, you have to get those old tenants in your mind to either change or move out.

Jesus gave a parable in Matthew 13:3-4 of a sower sowing seed. Some of the seed was eaten up by birds. He expounded, telling us that the seed is the Word of God that goes into the soil of your heart. Immediately the devil comes and tries to take it out of your heart. The devil would love to pluck the principles of wealth out of your heart and never let you put them into practice, to keep you at your current level financially. Satan wants you in the crummy hotel room on the first floor by the utility closet and ice machine. His goal is to keep you from realizing that you already have the key to the concierge level.

The first time I heard it taught that Christians should not be poor, everything in me rebelled because when I started in ministry I was sort of a hippie-like poverty preacher. I told my little con-

God has given you the key to the Wealthy Place.

gregation: "The big churches that have money and wealthy members are most likely not going to get into the Kingdom of Heaven." Then I would proceed to tell the story about the camel and the eye of the needle.

Then I learned from the Word of God that I was wrong. I changed my attitude (my mental tenants) and started preaching that God wants us to prosper, even when, at the time, it didn't look like I was prospering. I drove an absolute wreck of a car, beat up and held together with rope and duct tape. You could see me coming down the road a mile away because of the cloud of smoke. I had to carry extra cans of transmission fluid and a can opener with me to replace the fluid that was constantly leaking out because I couldn't afford a new transmission.

Nonetheless, those old mental tenants were starting to move out.

I kept preaching anti-poverty and pro-prosperity messages, and good things started happening. My paycheck was the same, but other avenues of blessing began to come into my life. For example, a guy came over and said, "Brother Williams, I have two nice sweaters here that my mother bought me, and I don't like them. You can have them." The same thing happened with a pair of shoes and a nice suit. God started blessing me because my attitude had changed.

You have the key to the concierge level of life.

Next a new refrigerator arrived, then an air conditioner, a piano, and the list of unusual blessings went on and on once I changed my beliefs about wealth; once I forced those old mental tenants to move out.

START WHERE YOU'RE AT

You may be thinking that God's many promises of wealth in the Old Testament don't apply under the new covenant. But God doesn't remove blessings when He adds more. He's a God of increase and multiplication, and every time there's an Old Testament promise, there's a New Testament Scripture to verify its validity under the new covenant. If, for instance, it says in Genesis that God made Abraham rich with livestock, silver and gold, then what He did for Abraham, our father in the faith, He'll do for us. God gives the seed, Isaiah 55 says. God gives the power, Deuteronomy 8:18 says. God gives the increase, 1 Corinthians 3:7 says. You and I simply have to activate these promises through faith and action.

> For as the rain cometh down, and the snow from heaven, and returneth not thither, but watereth the earth, and maketh it bring forth and bud, that it may give seed to the sower, and bread to the eater:
>
> So shall my word be that goeth forth out of my mouth: it shall not return unto me void, but it shall accomplish that which I please, and it shall prosper in the thing whereto I sent it.
>
> —Isaiah 55:10-11
>
> But thou shalt remember the LORD thy God: for it is he that giveth thee power to get wealth, that he may establish his covenant which he sware unto thy fathers, as it is this day.
>
> —Deuteronomy 8:18
>
> So then neither is he that planteth any thing, neither he that watereth; but God that giveth the increase.
>
> —1 Corinthians 3:7

There is a level in God's Spirit in the realm of prosperity, abundance, and overflow, riches and wealth that you can get to *if* you have the key. My prayer is that in reading this book, you come to understand *The Wealthy Place*. I'm not just talking about a house in the suburbs and a couple of cars. I'm talking about riches where you can write out a check for thousands of dollars to your favorite ministry — every week! And God will always supply abundantly so you'll have plenty for yourself and your family besides.

If you're living in a project or a housing development somewhere, it may seem impossible for you to own your own home or car someday. But I want to tell you that with God all things are possible, and the plan for you is in the Bible! Mark 10:30 says we'll have houses (plural). I believe God's plan for us isn't just to have one house, but several.

Why do you think Jesus said in John 14:2 that "in my Father's house are many mansions"? I think He wants us to quit thinking about shacks and two-bedroom, one-bath homes and start moving up to that concierge level where we don't even have to think about finances. We don't have to go to the store and wonder if we can afford certain items. We don't have to spend hours of precious time looking through the papers, finding and clipping out coupons, just to save a few dollars at the grocery store.

One time, years ago, I had saved up $300 to buy some suits at a famous suit store in Tulsa, where I had heard all the popular evangelists bought their suits. I got there, and this young gangster-looking salesman tried to sell me several suits, but they were all $900 to $1,600 each. I was so disappointed.

Later I was sitting in a meeting at Oral Roberts University. They were facing a crisis and needed to take an offering. God spoke to my heart and told me to give a hundred dollars, but I said, "I only have $5." He then reminded me of the suit money and prompted me to give $100 of it. So I did. Now I had only $200 dollars left for suits.

We left Tulsa without any new suits. I was disappointed, but when we got to St. Louis, Mary Jo and I saw a big sign that read "Men's Slack Outlet." Mary Jo pointed it out but I said, "Nah, I don't want to get off the highway." Then I thought better of it and went back. It was like a miracle. They had all these suits; wonderful, brand name suits and sports jackets that came to the clearance center because they were missing a button or some small thing. They even provided tailoring right on the spot and I bought five suits for less than $200. I was shouting hallelujahs all the way back to Lansing. That's the way it works when you start to come into *The Wealthy Place!*

Now, let's get into the foundational principles of wealth, leading up to the key principle that ties them all together.

*Lack and poverty
are not God's will for you
at any time.*

CHAPTER

GOD HATES POVERTY!

Commit with me right now to shoot for the highest level of wealth you can: the concierge level. Don't settle for the fourth or fifth floors, but aim for the top. That's where we're most effective for Christ, where our abundance allows us to manage greater things. Remember, when you properly manage the wealth God has entrusted to you, He multiplies the resources of wealth that flow into your life. In other words, you'll enjoy a whole lot more being a manager of a big account than being a manager of a small account. I'd rather be managing God's big accounts than God's little accounts. And the big accounts are found in *The Wealthy Place*.

We've seen the first principle: Wealth is meant primarily for the advancement of the Gospel of the Kingdom. The next principle of *The Wealthy Place* is this:

You must believe that lack and poverty are not God's will for you at any time.

You can resist prosperity and abundance, but if you resist it, you are resisting the will of God. In John 10:10a Jesus identified the devil and his mode of operation.

> **The thief cometh not, but for to steal, and to kill, and to destroy...**

He's stealing people's futures and they don't even know it. He's destroying their finances, killing their chances for the future. But 1 John 3:8 says Jesus came to destroy the works of the devil!

> **For this purpose the Son of God was manifested, that he might destroy the works of the devil.**
>
> **—1 John 3:8b**

Have you ever heard the phrase "Money can't buy happiness"? Do you know what that is? It's the poverty mentality speaking. Do you know what I say? I say *lack of money* doesn't bring happiness! Think about it. Money brings a lot more happiness than poverty. If you don't believe it, go down to the poverty-stricken sections of your town and observe all the "happiness" there. You'll see prostitution, drug-trafficking, shortened lives, peep shows, laziness, and crimes of all sorts.

Money brings a lot more happiness than poverty.

Then go to the areas where people are doing well, and you'll find that money brings a lot more happiness than poverty. Some say money brings problems, but I say there are more problems without money. If your hot-water heater breaks down and you don't have the money to get a new one, you have a problem don't you? Money can solve a lot of problems, and God understands that. That's why He put so much wealth at our fingertips. We need simply to be willing and obedient.

> Come now, and let us reason together, saith the LORD: though your sins be as scarlet, they shall be as white as snow; though they be red like crimson, they shall be as wool.
>
> If ye be willing and obedient, ye shall eat the good of the land:
> —Isaiah 1:18-19

Some people think there's glory in poverty, but I have been in poverty and I didn't see any glory. I saw crime, drug abuse, and violence up close. I have been to the slums of many major cities. I almost lost my life in the slums of Honolulu one night. If it hadn't been for a friend of mine, now an officer on the Detroit police force, who pulled me out of the way, my neck would have been sliced. I didn't see any glory that night, in the slums of America or any other nation, nor have I seen it since.

One of the devil's most devious lies is that poverty is a badge of honor and brings glory to God. "After all," he says, "look at all the people who made poverty vows and how holy they are today."

Listen! The Bible NEVER commands anybody to make a poverty vow — not once. That idea is unscriptural and comes from Eastern religions. It has nothing to do with biblical Christianity or even Judaism. Poverty, biblically, is never a badge of honor or glory but is *always* related to laziness, unbelief, or lack of knowledge. It is never related to the virtues the Bible identifies as the fruit of the Spirit. Glory and honor don't come out of slums until someone puts God's principles to work in their life and gets out of the slums.

Money can solve a lot of problems.

WEALTH WORKS!

Wherever God's covenant is, there is wealth and happiness. I went on a trip to Europe and Africa and discovered that the nations with a strong Christian influence are the nations that are, by and large, prospering relative to the nations around them. I visited Malawi and talked with people who had been in miracle crusades there. Their president at the time was a born-again Christian, and I was told that 60-70 percent of the population is born again. My traveling companions and I sensed such prosperity in that nation. There was wealth brimming up everywhere. It's not yet the wealth we know in the U.S., but compared to Mozambique, Sudan and some of the other nations of Africa, it was tremendous wealth.

God wants to establish His covenant, and wherever His covenant goes, prosperity follows!

I visited two socialist countries and sensed oppression, sadness, and poverty. They had the potential for wealth, but that potential was not realized. I know there is enough wealth on earth to go around for everyone, and you don't need to be a socialist to get the wealth distributed properly if everyone believes in and acts upon God's principles.

Wealth is a blessing, not a curse.

I met a traveling couple at a restaurant in Spain, and they appeared to be quite wealthy. They asked me, "How do you feel about wealth?" and I answered, "God thinks it's terrific. If He had His way, everybody in this world would be wealthy." They responded, "That can't be. There's not enough wealth for everybody." I answered, "God's got enough wealth for everybody, all six and one half billion of us."

POVERTY AS A DESTINY?

Some of you reading this book have the power to get wealth, but it lies dormant because you have been afraid to let it rise up from within you. You may be:

• Afraid you might displease God.

• Afraid you might backslide.

• Afraid the wealth might change you.

• Afraid somebody might criticize you.

Some Christians foolishly or ignorantly say, "Some were made to be wealthy and some were made to be poor, and I was one of those allotted in life to be poor." NO! God is no respecter of persons. The Bible says He made Abraham wealthy, and the Bible declared it to be a blessing. In Galatians we are told that Jesus Christ, when He died on the Cross, took us out from under the curse of the law and made us children of Abraham to share in the *same* blessings that Abraham enjoyed. Part of those blessings is wealth. Don't you see how basic it is?

> Christ hath redeemed us from the curse of the law, being made a curse for us: for it is written, Cursed is every one that hangeth on a tree:
>
> That the blessing of Abraham might come on the Gentiles through Jesus Christ; that we might receive the promise of the Spirit through faith.
>
> —Galatians 3:13-14
>
> Therefore it is of faith, that it might be by grace; to the end the promise might be sure to all the seed; not to that only which is of the law, but to that also which is of the faith of Abraham; who is the father of us all.
>
> —Romans 4:16

But the problem is lack of knowledge concerning wealth, so people go through life groping under the door to *The Wealthy Place*, grasping for money and wondering how to make ends meet. One lady said, "The love of money is the root of all evil, but I can't fall in love with my money because it doesn't stick around long enough for us to develop a relationship!" That's true of far too many people.

Poverty has no virtue whatsoever, neither does wealth. Having money doesn't make us godly, but the attitude of our heart does. Jesus said, "Seek ye first the Kingdom of God (Matthew 6:33)." He didn't say we're not to seek wealth, but that we're not to seek wealth first.

WEALTHY ON THE INSIDE

You have to be wealthy on the inside before you can be wealthy on the outside. I remember back in 1980 when the church board raised my pay to $125 a week from $25 a week. I was driving a 1973 Oldsmobile that had a worn-out transmission that smoked. I mentioned earlier that I carried a case of transmission fluid in my car with me because whenever I stopped, the transmission fluid would drain out. It was cheaper to go over to the discount store and buy a box of transmission fluid every week than to get the transmission fixed or to buy a new car. But I drove that smoking car down the street as if I were in a Rolls Royce.

My son went to Verlinden Elementary School where many of the poor kids went. One day he came home and whispered, "I found out there are a lot of poor kids in that school. I didn't tell them how rich we are because I didn't want them to feel bad." I was stone broke, but my children never knew it because I projected myself wealthy. Why? Because that was God's picture of me.

I took one year to search the Scriptures to find out what God said about wealth, riches, and prosperity. I'd heard all of the negative preachers, but after my full year of research I stopped believing them. I saw that God has pleasure in the prosperity of His servant.

> Let them shout for joy, and be glad, that favour my righteous cause: yea, let them say continually, Let the LORD be magnified, which hath pleasure in the prosperity of his servant.
>
> —Psalms 35:27

I remember stumbling upon an old $500 insurance policy I had purchased when I was in the Navy. I cashed it in and made my first investment. I was scared silly to invest, but I knew that if my family was going to prosper, God was going to have to show me some other ways because obviously the church board was not going to be my source. Over the years God did show me how to manage money properly. You'd probably faint if I told you what that $500 investment has grown to today—25 years later.

God is raising up people now who will flow in a ministry of wealth; people who live on the concierge level so they can advance the cause of the Gospel of Jesus Christ. *I believe you are one of them.* I believe every believer has the opportunity to be at least a millionaire and manage the planet's wealth for the glory of God.

> ...for then thou shalt make thy way prosperous, and then thou shalt have good success.
>
> —Joshua 1:8

> Being enriched in every thing to all bountifulness, which causeth through us thanksgiving to God.
>
> —2 Corinthians 9:11

In other words, God wants to give you much so you can give much! If you're poor, how can you give? It's only the educated who can help the uneducated. Only those who are in health can help the sick. Only the wealthy can help the poor. So why do people resist? Let's find out.

*God wants your needs
to be met, but He wants much
more that that!*

CHAPTER 6

FEAR OF THE WEALTHY PLACE

Let's delve deeper into this fear of money that traps people in mediocre living. Some think money is filthy and that poverty is glorious. But money is neutral, like fire. You can use fire for heat or arson.

The point is that you must become a trustworthy manager of money.

The devil desperately tries to block this. He breeds bad attitudes about money. He has an aggressive policy of containment toward God's people. Psalm 24:1 says:

> The earth is the LORD'S, and the fulness thereof; the world, and they that dwell therein.

What does the psalmist mean by "the earth?" Simply this: the earth is real estate. And God owns it all! But the devil is fighting tooth and nail to control as much as he can; however, he can only do it with the consent of man. Whenever a church expands or builds, the devil lays his strategy to contain it.

If God owns the real estate, doesn't it make sense that He would want His children, not the raunchy video store owner, to own it? We've not been aggressive enough with the devil in taking and possessing property. I don't mean taking it by physical force, but expanding our borders, making honest and shrewd business deals, creating wealth as the body of Christ and using it to grow the square footage of God-honoring properties in our cities.

Criticism is the loveless tool of the unmotivated.

Every positive move forward takes assertiveness. If you get a raise, the devil may try to contain you by flattening your tires. If you decide to pray more, the devil may try to get you to fall asleep instead. If your church builds, you can expect some of hell's characters to show up like mobsters out of a bad Mafia movie causing trouble or stirring the pot wherever they can to turn people against each other.

Moving beyond the devil's containment takes vigorous effort and spiritual energy! I'm not content to stay the same tomorrow as I am today. I'm not content with my bankroll, my influence, my ministry. I'm no longer content on the third and fourth floors when way up on top is *The Wealthy Place.*

> And from the days of John the Baptist until now the
> kingdom of heaven suffereth violence, and the violent
> take it by force.
> —Matthew 11:12

Yes, we need to take it by force, but some people—perhaps you—are paralyzed by fear. What are some fears and criticisms people project about money?

❏ NUMBER ONE: "I'M AFRAID PEOPLE WILL CRITICIZE ME."

Mention money in church, and you are liable to be shushed up by people who say, "Money ought not be discussed in church. If the church needs money, we should pray more." There is truth in that, but it also implies that we shouldn't use any of the other tools God has given us to solve money problems. The instant reaction of many Christians is that money is evil. That's the way they've been trained to think.

There are 700 direct references to money in the Bible. Two-thirds of Jesus' parables dealt with money. Mark 10:30 says:

> But he shall receive an hundredfold now in this time,
> houses, and brethren, and sisters, and mothers, and chil-
> dren, and lands, with persecutions; and in the world to
> come eternal life.

Don't worry about the criticism and persecution. The higher up you go in the elevator of life, the fewer people there are that live on that floor. Jesus promised that when you prosper, you'll get persecution right along with it.

Why are some people so critical of money when God clearly says Heaven will be a place of great wealth? If God was critical of wealth, why are His streets constructed with gold? Why does He speak of treasures in Heaven?

The thing we should criticize is the wrong, immature, unhealthy attitudes about money that keep believers in bondage. When we learn principles of giving, receiving, budgeting, saving and investing, then money will flow to us *in the healthy way God intended!*

When I fly, I ride first class almost all the time. If Mary Jo is with me, I have to ride coach because she doesn't have the elite card I have. I almost always get upgraded. I pay coach, but I ride first class. One time I bought Mary Jo an upgrade to first class so she could ride with me. In the Detroit airport we bumped into a family that used to come to our church. They explained they didn't go to church anymore because they had so much going on; getting an education, working a lot of hours, and everything. They had the classic first-floor mentality. They had embraced a type of overworking poverty.

When our flight was announced for boarding, Mary Jo and I found our first-class seats, and a little while later all the people in coach began boarding the plane. This couple came on, saw us and said, "That's not fair. You get to ride in first class and we're way in the back."

I fly 100,000 miles a year with Northwest Airlines, earning the right to ride first class. But beyond that, her envy showed an attitude of lack. It was as if I could see her reaching under the door to *The Wealthy Place* to snag a few dollars of wealth and drag them back to "The Mediocre Room" she lived in. I wanted to tell her, "You'll always ride in the tail of the plane until you change your attitude," but I didn't.

Criticism is the loveless tool of the unmotivated. Critics usually do the least amount of work, point out the most problems, and never become a part of the solution. They appoint themselves the accuser, judge, jury, and executioner. Critics will criticize no matter what you do. I used to drive a subcompact car and people criticized me saying, "You make the church look bad." I bought a luxurious Oldsmobile and people said, "Stay away from that church, the pastor drives a big luxury car." I couldn't do right!

Don't worry about persecution. Expect it! Then when it comes, you'll laugh and shrug it off.

❏ NUMBER TWO: "MAKING MONEY IS DISHONEST."

Have you ever heard somebody say, "I'm too honest to be wealthy"? That statement is incredibly shallow. It presupposes that all wealthy people are dishonest and the person making the statement is the epitome of purity. People who legitimately become wealthy almost always possess great integrity and honesty. They are generally people who have honor. It's miserly, greedy people who tend to cut corners and deal dishonestly, hoping to preserve the little they have.

❏ NUMBER THREE: "I DON'T NEED MORE MONEY. I'M HAPPY IF MY NEEDS ARE MET."

When someone says this, Satan has scored again. This attitude focuses on self and makes satisfying our needs the chief aim of money, but that isn't how God sees it. It may seem pious to say we will be content if our needs are met, but implicit in that attitude is the statement, "Forget missions, the church, the poor, the hungry, as long as my needs are met. I don't need to develop skills or activate my God-given power to get wealth because I'm satisfied with my current level." Pure selfishness!

Yes, God wants your needs to be met, but He wants much more than that! He wants to give you enough so you can give it away.

What would you do with "extra" money? Print Bibles for overseas missions? Support a missionary? Help your church build a new sanctuary or facility large enough to hold the lost souls you expect to come in? Christians have a responsibility to make all the money they can, legitimately and honestly, so they can bless God's work with it.

Dream a little! Think what you'd do if you had the financial wherewithal. Quit focusing on your own paltry needs. Those are secondary to the Kingdom.

❏ NUMBER FOUR: "I MIGHT BACKSLIDE IF I ATTAIN WEALTH."

A statement like this shows that a person might *already* be backsliding. If money is going to cause someone to backslide, that only reveals their true commitment, as if they're barely hanging on to faith as it is, and money is the villain who grinds its heel into their fingers and sends them over the cliff.

If money can make you backslide, anything can make you backslide!

❏ NUMBER FIVE: "I'M ALREADY WEALTHIER THAN MOST PEOPLE IN THE WORLD."

Almost any North American or Western European would be considered vastly wealthy by comparison to a citizen from most other countries. In Bangladesh the average salary is less than $100 a year. I met a man overseas who made $20 a month. Compared to him we're already rich. Most of America's poor people own cars, televisions, and live in air-conditioned apartments or houses.

My answer to this argument is that we don't live in Bangladesh or a Third World country. We live in North America or Western Europe—that is where God has placed you and me. To whom much is given, much is required. God has given us great wealth so we can help other countries and spread the Gospel. It's a treasonous cop-out to reject wealth and let it go into the hands of someone who doesn't pursue God's purposes with it.

Have you ever considered how much wealth there is in the world and how much wealth people are laying up for themselves? The former Shah of Iran had enough money to give $3,330,000 to every man, women, boy and girl in my city of Lansing, Michigan, and still have plenty of money left over for himself. And that's just one rich man!

We are led to believe that there isn't enough wealth to go around in the world. Every person on Planet Earth could have a bank account of over a million dollars if all the wealth were divided equally. And we still wouldn't be out of wealth!

Wealth isn't as scarce on this earth as some try to make us think. Even India, a "poor" country, has enough wealth to feed every man, woman, and child in the nation. India doesn't have a poverty problem; India has a religion problem. If they would feed their people what they feed their cows, their people would not be hungry. But the covenant of God isn't established in Hinduism, it's established in Jesus Christ.

If you've accepted any of these lies, make a conscious effort to recognize them and toss them out of your mental apartment building. They are problem tenants, so treat them accordingly.

Next we'll see the other side of the coin—what God thinks when we start to attain wealth and use it wisely.

I*f there is so much opulence, extravagance, and outrageous wealth in Heaven, then it is God's will for His children on the earth!*

CHAPTER 7

YOUR PROSPERITY BRINGS GOD PLEASURE!

God absolutely wants you blessed with wealth, and your prosperity brings Him great pleasure. You've read the Scripture that says the Lord hath pleasure in the prosperity of His servant. The book of Revelation tells us that we were put here for His pleasure. One of the ways of bringing pleasure to God is by prospering. It's so simple, it goes right over most people's heads.

> ...Let the LORD be magnified, which hath pleasure in the prosperity of his servant.
>
> —Psalm 35:27c

> **Thou art worthy, O Lord, to receive glory and honour and power: for thou hast created all things, and for thy pleasure they are and were created.**
>
> —**Revelation 4:11 (Italics Added)**

It's simple. We were created for God's pleasure and when we prosper, it brings Him pleasure.

This chapter is about making sure you get this foundational principle!

> **A land wherein thou shalt eat bread without scarceness, thou shalt not lack any thing in it...**
>
> —**Deuteronomy 8:9a**

In Deuteronomy 8, God tells His people His will, desire and purpose for them. One of the first things He says is, "I'm going to bring you to a land wherein thou shalt eat bread without scarceness." You know what it's like when you want a sandwich and the bread drawer is empty. It happens to me sometimes. I want a sandwich. I go to the bread drawer, and the only thing in there are Mary Jo's rice crackers. I don't want a rice cracker. I want a hunk of bread for my peanut butter or lean roast turkey.

Jesus became poor by Heaven's standards so you and I could become rich by earth's standards.

In the place God wants to bring you, you're not going to lack any food. You'll eat the best of the land.

> If you will only let me help you, if you will only obey, then I will make you rich!
> —Isaiah 1:19 (TLB)

I used to think poor, fat people wouldn't be so poor if they ate less. Then it occurred to me that poor people eat a lot of cheap food: macaroni and cheese, (four boxes for a dollar). It's all starch, which packs on the pounds. It's not healthy to be poor.

Have you ever been at the end of your money and the furnace broke down? You wondered how to get it repaired. There was no money in the bank and the car payment was due. The credit card payment was due. The book-of-the-month club payment was due. So you put the furnace repair on your credit card, and by the time you ended up paying it off, the interest cost you more than the repair.

DON'T FORGET!

God says in Deuteronomy 8, verses 11 and 12 to:

> Beware that thou forget not the LORD thy God, in not keeping his commandments, and his judgments, and his statutes, which I command thee this day: Lest when thou hast eaten and art full, and hast built goodly houses, and dwelt therein.

Jesus said something similar in John 14: "I go to prepare a place for you; in My Father's house there are many mansions." What if He'd said, "In My Father's house are many pup tents, shanties, and shacks?" He didn't. He was trying to yank us up to a different level of thinking, to show us the lavishness of God and the opulence of Heaven.

We pray, "Thy Kingdom come, Thy will be done in earth as it is in Heaven." If there is so much opulence, extravagance, and outrageous wealth in Heaven, then it is God's will for His children on the Earth!

> Lest when thou hast eaten and art full, and hast built goodly houses, and dwelt therein; And when thy herds and thy flocks multiply...
>
> —Deuteronomy 8:12-13a

That's talking about your productivity. This next part is for all those who say the Bible only talks about spiritual wealth. Silver and gold refer to financial wealth.

> ...and thy silver and thy gold is multiplied, and all that thou hast is multiplied.
>
> —Deuteronomy 8:13b

I love that word "multiplied."

Are you into multiplication? If you made $10,000 last year, are you making $20,000 this year? $40,000 next year; $80,000 the next year; $160,000 the next year; $320,000 the next year; $640,000 the next year; and $1.2 million the next year? Are you into that kind of multiplication? That's what He's talking about here. He said everything you have is to be multiplied.

Verse 18 begins:

> But thou shalt remember the LORD thy God: for it is he that giveth thee power to get wealth, that he may establish his covenant which he sware unto thy fathers, as it is this day.

Paul said all the promises of God are "yes" and "amen" in Christ Jesus (2 Corinthians 1:20). All the statements and promises that God made to His people under the old covenant are good for us today. Jesus is the Mediator of a better covenant because, as believers, we can enjoy the promises of blessings of both covenants, without the curses of the old covenant.

> But now hath he obtained a more excellent ministry, by how much also he is the mediator of a better covenant, which was established upon better promises.
>
> —Hebrews 8:6

Verse 18 continues:

> ...it is he that giveth thee POWER TO GET WEALTH.

Notice He didn't say skill, education, or talent. I don't care if you're a kindergarten dropout. If you're in Christ Jesus, He has given you the *power* to get wealth. I don't care if you feel like you're the stupidest person in class, He's given you power! It doesn't take skill, education, talent, or capabilities to get wealth—it takes power. There's a big difference.

JESUS PAID THE PRICE

I get upset with preachers who falsely spiritualize simple truths. This next Scripture tells how Jesus Christ became poor so that you could become rich.

> For ye know the grace of our Lord Jesus Christ, that, though he was rich, yet for your sakes he became poor, that ye through his poverty might be rich.
>
> —2 Corinthians 8:9

Some preachers try to say that this only means spiritual riches. I thank God for spiritual riches. But to use that kind of logic you'd have to say Jesus became poor spiritually so that I could become rich spiritually.

Jesus became poor by Heaven's standards so you and I could become rich by earth's standards.

Did Jesus become poor spiritually? Of course not! That's almost blasphemous to even suggest. Rather, He became poor by Heaven's standards so you and I could become rich by earth's standards. You see, the very first thing Jesus said when He quoted from Isaiah in Luke 4:18a was:

"The Spirit of the Lord is upon me, because he hath anointed me to preach the gospel to the poor."

What is the Gospel (or Good News) to the poor? "Brother, be content in the situation you're in." "Someday, in the by and by, you'll get your mansion over there in glory if you hold on long enough." No! The Good News to the poor is, "You don't have to be poor! Jesus paid the price to deliver you from sin, sickness, disease, *and* poverty."

> The LORD shall open unto thee his good treasure, the heaven to give the rain unto thy land in his season, and to bless all the work of thine hand: and thou shalt lend unto many nations, and thou shalt not borrow.

> And the LORD shall make thee the head, and not the
> tail; and thou shalt be above only, and thou shalt not be
> beneath; if that thou hearken unto the commandments
> of the LORD thy God, which I command thee this day,
> to observe and to do them.
>
> —Deuteronomy 28:12-13

God blesses us with the power to get wealth, and your prosperity brings Him pleasure (Psalm 35 tells us that). Deuteronomy 8:18 says He gives you power to get wealth. Deuteronomy 28 says you should be the lender and not the borrower; the head, not the tail.

Having settled that, let's get into the nuts and bolts of building wealth, beginning by removing wrong belief systems that keep people out of *The Wealthy Place.*

No *believer on the planet has a money problem.*

CHAPTER

THERE'S NO SUCH THING AS A MONEY PROBLEM

People often say, "Pray for me. I'm having financial problems." No, they have another problem. It's a solid fact: *No believer on the planet has a money problem.*

They may have an obedience problem which is ultimately a faith problem.

Or, they may have an attitude problem.

Or, they may have a vision problem.

For God's children, there's no such thing as a money problem. It's always an obedience, vision or attitude problem.

Rick McDermott, a member of our church in Lansing,

was a drug addict in Hawaii. Years ago a young lady named Michelle, a missionary with Youth With a Mission, shared the love of Jesus with him as he staggered down a street in Hawaii. Rick accepted Christ, went through Teen Challenge for a year, then moved to Lansing and became part of our church.

I remember Rick being in my leadership class and stopping me after class. He asked for prayer because he was trying to launch a painting business but couldn't get anyone to hire him. We prayed, and I told him to plant a seed. He didn't have much, but he planted a money seed into God's work anyway.

Afterward, God gave him an idea. There was a contractor in our church who built quality, upscale houses. Rick went to him and said, "Let me paint the houses for you, inside and out. I won't charge you anything unless you like my work. Then you can pay me whatever you want." Rick went out to a half-million dollar home, painted it and didn't charge anything. His work was superb, so the contractor paid him and started referring him to other builders and contractors. Soon Rick was getting jobs everywhere. As his business skyrocketed he started hiring Teen Challenge graduates — former drug addicts — as employees.

Your attitude toward money will be money's attitude toward you.

One night God woke him up at 3 a.m. and told him to buy a car for a certain person. Rick didn't have much to give, but he obeyed and went to a used car lot, but the Lord told him to make it a new car. Rick bought a $20,000 car and gave it away the next day. The very next week he got a call from a drugstore chain in Indiana. The owner decided he wanted all the drugstores and warehouses painted. Rick bid on the job and won. In two weeks, he made $250,000.

For God's children, there's no such thing as a money problem. It's always an obedience, vision or attitude problem.

God always asks you to do something radical before He does something radical for you. What if Rick hadn't given that car when God told him to? Do you think Rick wants that $20,000 back that he planted? Of course not.

The next week he got a call for a job in Texas. Rick didn't really want to go to Texas so he named a big price. They said, "Okay, we're flying you out — first class." He went and made another $250,000. Today he has one of the top painting companies in Michigan. All this in less than seven years!

God's will is wealth, but He wants us to be as radical as He is! Every one of God's children could easily be a millionaire in 20 years or less, because when God does it, it's a miraculous thing. It doesn't take forever to get us out from where we are and into *The Wealthy Place* once we learn radical obedience.

ATTITUDE CHECK

Prosperity isn't always about money. It starts with your attitude. You have to have an attitude toward money before money gets an attitude toward you. In fact, your attitude toward money will be money's attitude toward you. If you have an attitude that money is nothing but filthy lucre, that's what money's attitude toward you is going to be.

God always asks you to do something radical before He does something radical for you.

Years ago when my little son asked if we could go to Dairy Queen and we had hardly any money, I told him, "I have a better idea. I'll teach you how to whittle a stick." That seemed so cool, he forgot all about Dairy Queen. I never once told my kids we couldn't afford something.

The challenge is attitude. We talked earlier about the poverty attitude and the fear of *The Wealthy Place*. Jesus said, "Out of the abundance of the heart, the mouth speaks" (Matthew 12:34). Your attitude toward money (and anything else) is going to be known by your words. Phrases like, "Do you kids think money grows on trees?" or "We just can't afford it" indicate a poverty attitude.

When I was earning $125 a week as a pastor at Mount Hope Church, it took two weeks' pay just to make the house payment. But I didn't go around telling everyone how broke I was. I wasn't poor because I wasn't poor in my attitude.

Here's a quick test to help you identify a poverty attitude:

1. What is your first reaction to the Scripture, "Beloved, I wish above all things that thou mayest prosper and be in health even as thy soul prospereth" (3 John 2)?

   ❑ a. I must have read that wrong. It can't *really* say that because God doesn't believe in prosperity.

   ❑ b. I'm sure this was true in the days of the apostles, but God's wishes have changed since the apostles died.

   ❑ c. I am loved by God, and He actually wants me to prosper.

2. When you face a financial trial, what do you find yourself saying?

   ❑ a. God caused this problem to teach me a lesson.

   ❑ b. It was not my fault, of course. It was the leaders in Washington that caused all of my problems.

   ❑ c. Well, I blew it somewhere. I'd better find out how to get up and get back on the move.

3. When you see wealthy people, what do you think?

   ❑ a. They must be using God's principles.

❑ b. They must be crooks.

4. When you see a poor person, what comes to your mind?

❑ a. It's his own foolish fault.

❑ b. Thank God I'm not a low-class bum like that.

❑ c. God loves him and so do I. I should help
him somehow.

5. When one of your friends or peers gets a new house, car,
or major appliance of some sort, what are the first
thoughts that cross your mind?

❑ a. Praise the Lord, they deserve it.

❑ b. I wonder where they got the money for that?

❑ c. Well hardy-har-har, I hope it falls apart.

❑ d. I wonder why I couldn't get one, only a better, more
expensive one.

Can you figure out the right answers? I bet you can, using
what we've learned already.

SIGNS OF AN OWNERSHIP ATTITUDE

When you have a wrong attitude, it often shows itself as
an attitude of "ownership" which is a sin. Psalm 24:1 says,
"The earth is the Lord's and the fullness thereof." God owns
it. The clothes I'm wearing now aren't mine. God owns them.
I'm a manager of what God has entrusted to me. If God says
to give something away, it has to go.

If a person has a sinful love for money, it usually shows up in worries about money. He thinks, "When I have a stockpile of $6 million, I won't worry anymore." Listen, if you worry about $6, you'll worry about $60. If you worry about $60, you'll worry about $600. And think how worried you'd be if you had $6 million or even $6 billion!

An owner worries; a manager rejoices. If God owns it, it's up to Him to protect it. It's only up to me to manage it. And I like managing, because God lets me keep a percentage. If you manage a movie star's career, you get to keep 15 percent of his or her earnings. But if you manage God's money, He lets you keep up to 90 percent!

Thinking that God is stingy is another indication of the sinful attitude of ownership. I remember a missionary who stood in the pulpit at my church one time. In the first service he said, "God, deliver us in America from the spirit of prosperity." And then he slapped his hand down on the pulpit and blurted out, "Damn prosperity!" I knew he was really talking about covetousness and greed, because prosperity is a beautiful, biblical word. Prosperity is one of God's blessings on a person's life. Don't damn God's blessings. Don't say, "Deliver us from the blessings of God." I had an associate minister talk to him between services. This minister, a bodybuilder, walked up to him and said, "Hey! Don't damn prosperity in the next service." And he didn't!

POOR-MOUTHING

I've talked about this already, but it's worth repeating that poor-mouthing is a sign of a wrong attitude. "Oh, I could never afford that." Remember? Your mind is hearing you say that, and your mind goes to work to fulfill that dire prophecy.

Mary Jo and I used to live below the national poverty level. One year I made $6,250 and the next year I made $7,000, so at least I was headed in the right direction. And we were giving 20 percent of our income to God. We were, on one occasion, down to crackers and a little tiny bit of milk. But we never told the kids we were poor, and we never acted like it was a permanent state for us. We wanted to get up to the concierge level, and by God's grace, we have.

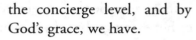

The Wealthy Place has to be a revelation and an attitude of the soul before it becomes a physical reality.

But poor-mouthing could have kept us in the hole of poverty if we had succumbed to it. In 1987 our state-wide office needed a new district building. The one we owned was run down and in a deteriorating area of town. That year at a district council meeting, the superintendent announced he was taking an offering for a new building. I whipped out the checkbook and wrote a check, even though it was beyond what I thought I could afford. I was happy because we were on our way to getting a new district office. The pastor sitting behind me griped, "All they do is take offerings at district council. If it isn't for missions, it's for building a new district office or the campgrounds."

I thought, how many scores of kids are saved and filled with the Holy Spirit at our camps every year? What a blessing it is to support them. This griping pastor irritated me, but I didn't say anything to him.

You have the Abundant One living inside you.

A couple of months later, this same pastor and I were in a meeting together and I asked, "How's your church going?"

"Not very well," he said.

"What do you mean?"

"We can't get commitment out of the members. One week there'll be 75 people in church, the next week 27. And we don't have the money to do anything we want to do. We're not like you. Everything good happens to you over there in Lansing."

My mind flashed back to that district office offering. He was the guy complaining about the offering.

Do you know what I thought? He's right. Good things are always happening to Dave and Mary Jo Williams. Good things are always happening to Mount Hope Church. Why? Because we developed the right attitudes about money, and money is what builds a church's facilities.

RIGHT ATTITUDE

So, what *is* the right attitude to have toward money?

❏ **NUMBER ONE:** God gives me the power to get wealth. (Deuteronomy 8:18)

❏ **NUMBER TWO:** God wants me to enjoy good things. (1 Timothy 6:17)

❏ **NUMBER THREE:** God owns it all; I'm just a manager. (Matthew 25:14-30)

❏ **NUMBER FOUR:** God wishes that I prosper. (3 John 2)

❏ **NUMBER FIVE:** God promises to add wealth unto me as I seek first His Kingdom. (Matthew 6:33)

CAN GOD TRUST YOU WITH WEALTH?

Here's how God can trust you. First, you obey Him and adopt the attitude that you were not designed to be poor, broke, in debt, or lacking in any good thing. Jesus Christ came to give you the abundant life and you have the Abundant One living inside you. When you really understand and believe that abundance is on the inside of you, it starts to come out and you don't even know how.

You might say, "Dave, you're a preacher. Everybody wants to bless the preacher." Well, that's not been my experience! When our treasurer begrudgingly handed me my first paycheck for one week of full-time work at the church he whined,

"I don't know why we should be paying you, but here you are...I guess." He handed me a check for $25 after I'd spent the week visiting cranky people, sitting in that office eight hours a day talking to immature, grown-up brats who dropped in with loads of problems and no faith. I'd pray for them, and before I could say, "Amen" they'd interrupt and say, "And another thing..."

Don't you love that? What's the use of praying? They're not going to get anything from God because they're double-minded. The double-minded person can receive nothing from the Lord. They just want to whine. They cancel the law of prosperity in their lives.

> But let him ask in faith, nothing wavering. For he that wavereth is like a wave of the sea driven with the wind and tossed. For let not that man think that he shall receive any thing of the Lord. A double minded man is unstable in all his ways.
>
> —James 1:6-8

GRATITUDE — A KEY TO WEALTH

Another one of the keys to prosperity is gratitude. That is thanking God for everything you have. Thanking God that you're on level one, or two, or three. No, you may not be at the concierge level yet, but you are on your way!

Some people grumble and say, "All the church wants is my money." But I've never heard anyone say, "All the local casino wants is my money." You never hear anyone say, "All Colgate Palmolive wants is my money." "All that grocery store wants is my money." It's always someone with a poverty attitude who whines, "All that church wants is my money." If you listen too long to those who are bound for poverty, they'll probably drag you down with them. If those grumblers gain any wealth at all, it's going to fly away like a bird.

The Wealthy Place has to be a revelation and an attitude of the soul before it becomes a physical reality. It has to thrive as a vision in your soul before it can manifest in the natural. We'll talk about that next.

According to the Bible, you are absolutely, outrageously wealthy. When you have no physical evidence to that fact, you must use faith.

CHAPTER 9

FIXING YOUR VISION PROBLEM

Some people think God loves only the poor and destitute. He does love them incredibly but He also has many wealthy friends. Yes, you can be wealthy and be a friend of God too.

Abraham was a billionaire, and he was God's friend. Jesus said, "I don't call you servants anymore" (John 15:15). "I call you friends!" If Abraham was a billionaire and he was a friend of God and I'm a friend of the Son of God, then I ought to be at least a millionaire several times over, if not a billionaire.

THE EVIDENCE IS IN: YOU ARE A MILLIONAIRE!

You actually have, right now, evidence that you are a millionaire.

The evidence is this: according to the Bible, you are absolutely, outrageously wealthy. So, when you have no physical evidence to that fact, you must use faith as your evidence.

> **Now faith is the substance of things hoped for, the evidence of things not seen.**
>
> —Hebrews 11:1

The wealth that God gives isn't contingent upon the economy, quarterly earnings, the stock market, interest rates, or so-called economic indicators.

Let me lift your vision a little bit to what God wants to do through you.

Deuteronomy 2:7 says, *"...you shall have no lack even in desperate circumstances."*

Psalm 23:1 says, *"...the Lord is your shepherd, you shall lack nothing."*

Psalm 112:1-3 says, *"...wealth and riches shall be in your house, if you reverence the Lord."*

BREATH-TAKING WEALTH

1 Kings 10 tells us:

> And when the queen of Sheba heard of the fame of Solomon concerning the name of the LORD, she came to prove him with hard questions.

This queen from another land saw something in Solomon that made her curious, so she came to Jerusalem with a great entourage of servants and camels that bore spices and gold and precious stones. Here she was, a sinner, and she brought wealth to Solomon who was already wealthy.

> ... and when she was come to Solomon, she communed with him of all that was in her heart.

That means she bared her heart to Solomon. She was facing some kind of distress and wanted to talk to somebody who knew the Lord.

> ... there was not any thing hid from the king...

He was apparently flowing in the supernatural. He had divine words of knowledge concerning her distress.

> ... which he told her not. And when the queen of Sheba had seen all Solomon's wisdom, and the house that he had built, and the meat of his table, and the sitting of his servants, and the attendance of his ministers, and their apparel, and his cupbearers, and his ascent by which he went up unto the house of the LORD; there was no more spirit in her.

Solomon's wealth — his style, his clothes, his wisdom, his leadership — it all took her breath away.

And she said to the king:

> It was a true report that I heard in mine own land of thy acts and of thy wisdom. Howbeit I believed not the words, until I came, and mine eyes had seen it: and, behold, the half was not told me: thy wisdom and prosperity exceedeth the fame which I heard. Happy are thy men, happy are these thy servants, which stand continually before thee, and that hear thy wisdom.

Sure they were happy; they were getting paid a good salary! We could interpret it like this, "Happy are your assistants — your associates, — your secretaries, bookkeepers, and employees."

> Blessed be the LORD thy God, which delighted in thee to set thee on his throne, to be king for the LORD thy God: because thy God loved Israel, to establish them for ever, therefore made he thee king over them, to do judgment and justice.
>
> —2 Chronicles 9:8

And what did the queen of Sheba do?

She gave the king 120 talents of gold.

Plant your financial seeds into good ground.

That's eight tons, which would be approximately $83 million today. Solomon didn't need that. But do you know what? You don't give just because there's a need. You give where God tells you to give, and you give into a life or ministry that has the kind of anointing and blessings you want. I believe she wanted to plant her financial seed somewhere that would produce a good harvest for herself.

PLANT SEEDS WHEN YOU HAVE NEEDS

I know a man who had serious moral problems and multiple marriages. Then a distant relative died and left him a million dollars. He decided to get his life together, ordain himself and start a church. So he went and bought a church, ordained himself and started a religious sect, and went on television.

Less than three years later, he was flat broke. The million dollars was gone, his ministry didn't take off. Now he's going from church to church begging for money for his ministry. Do you think I want to plant my financial seed into a loser? I don't want a harvest of "loserdom" coming my way. I want a harvest of wealth. When I plant my seed, I expect a return, so I plant into winning soil, so-to-speak.

I've always believed in planting seeds when you have needs. Some people say they can't afford to plant financial seeds. I say you can't afford not to!

In Michigan, we built and established Gilead Healing Center, a beautiful multimillion-dollar healing complex with complete medical and care facilities. The most expensive part of supplying Gilead was the medical equipment. A single machine costs tens of thousands of dollars. Even the exam tables are incredibly expensive.

Our board agreed that we needed to plant a seed for Gilead. We took church money and planted a big financial seed into another ministry. Not long after that, the Blue Care Network closed a couple of their clinics around Lansing. The chief surgeon came to us, and God obviously gave us favor with him. He donated more than $2 million worth of medical equipment that

When I plant my seed, I expect a return, so I plant into winning soil, so-to-speak.

had barely been used! Some of it was brand new, still in the boxes. We had so much equipment we were even able to supply Dave Roever's medical clinics in Vietnam.

How do things like that happen? Simple! We planted a financial seed when we had a financial need. This should be just as common as breathing, because God has given us a plan for radical wealth in His Word.

Get a vision for wealth! The wealth that God gives isn't contingent upon the economy, quarterly earnings, the stock market, interest rates, or so-called economic indicators.

Get a vision for wealth!

In John 21 the disciples had been fishing all night and had caught nothing, but one word from Jesus — "throw the net on the other side of the boat" — brought them prosperity (John 21:6). The children of Israel received the wealth of Egypt in one day (Exodus 12:35-36)!

One word from Jesus can do the same in your life! I don't care how dry the economy is. Aimee Semple McPherson built Angelus Temple during the Great Depression. Everyone wondered how she did it. She did it by using God's economic system! God's people prosper when the economy is good *and* bad — when the market is up, down, or sideways.

We are now ready to learn the one unifying principle that ties all these others together and leads you to *The Wealthy Place.*

Y*ou must fully come out
of the mediocre place before
you can fully enter
The Wealthy Place.*

CHAPTER 10

GOING OUT AND COMING INTO

Are you ready for one of the greatest mysteries of life? Every person must understand this basic principle to go from lower-level living to the concierge level! Here it is.

You have to go OUT before you can come INTO.

You ask, "What does that mean?"

I'll tell you. Most people try to get wealth out of *The Wealthy Place* and pull it into their mediocre, disobedient lives. They aren't deliberately disobedient, but they're trying to live wealthy and mediocre at the same time — holding onto the mediocre mindset of the past.

You cannot be in two rooms at once. You have to leave one room to enter another. But many Christians try to get into

The Wealthy Place without leaving the mediocre place. They hold on to dead principles or try to blend them with wealth principles. It doesn't work. The principles of mediocrity and poverty deactivate the principles of wealth. *You must fully come out of the mediocre place before you can fully enter The Wealthy Place.*

When you let go of what's in your hand, God lets go of what's in His hand.

In the next few chapters I am going to share with you three principles to help explain what I mean about going *out* and coming *into.* Once you understand this, you won't have to make bigger demands on your boss, get a home equity loan, refinance your house, or work harder. You will find yourself in a place where money chases you.

> Thou hast caused men to ride over our heads; we went through fire and through water: but thou broughtest us out into a wealthy place.
>
> —Psalm 66:12

D-I-D

Here's an easy way to remember the principles I'm about to share: D-I-D. Each letter stands for something you need to come out of. I never want you to forget those three letters: D-I-D.

The First "D": Come Out Of "Disobedience"

Disobedience is a huge stumbling block to some Christians. It keeps many on the lower levels of life — in the poor rooms. The first test of financial obedience is the tithe. I meet so many professing believers who have weird concepts about the tithe. They're all poor or overworking. They say, "I didn't pay my tithe this week." Stop! They're wrong right there. It never was *their* tithe. God gives everybody 10 percent more than they really deserve or need. He does this as a test. Leviticus 27:30 says the tithe is the Lord's, not ours.

What is the tithe? It is ten percent of whatever your gross income or increase is. Income is what your gross pay is. Increase is what you gained in stocks, bank accounts and interest.

Will a man rob God? Yet ye have robbed me. But ye say, Wherein have we robbed thee? In tithes and offerings.

Ye are cursed with a curse: for ye have robbed me, even this whole nation.

Bring ye all the tithes into the storehouse, that there may be meat in mine house, and prove me now herewith, saith the LORD of hosts, if I will not open you the windows of heaven, and pour you out a blessing, that there shall not be room enough to receive it.

And I will rebuke the devourer for your sakes, and he shall not destroy the fruits of your ground; neither shall your vine cast her fruit before the time in the field, saith the LORD of hosts.

And all nations shall call you blessed: for ye shall be a delightsome land, saith the LORD of hosts.

—Malachi 3:8-12

Malachi 3:8-12 says that obedience in the tithe will do some powerful things in a person's life. First, it opens the windows of Heaven. You see, if a person or family isn't tithing, the windows of Heaven are not open to that person or family. Thus, the blessing of favor cannot come.

Second, the devourer is rebuked over our homes on our behalf.

I believe, according to Luke 6:38, that tithing opens the windows of Heaven, and offerings provide the measure whereby we can catch the blessings that are being poured out. If we tithe, the windows of Heaven open. But if we go a step further and give offerings (above and beyond the 10%), then God fulfills what He said in Luke 6:38:

"Give and it shall be given unto you, good measure, pressed down, shaken together and running over shall men give unto your bosom."

Normally people stop reading right there, but there's more:

"For with the same measure that ye mete withal it shall be measured to you again."

Some wonder why they are not very blessed. It's usually because they are stingy with God. They give tithes and think they've done a great service to God. God said you could rob him in two ways, one is in tithes and the other is in offerings.

Some use teaspoons in their giving, some wheelbarrows, some dump trucks to give, and God compensates them accordingly.

Whenever I start feeling greedy or I find myself thinking too much about money matters, I begin to "violently" give. I write the biggest check I can and put it in the offering. I don't like to waste time on greed, so I get extreme. That's what the poor woman did the day Jesus was watching people put money into the treasury. She gave two mites, all she had, and did violence against the devil's greed. She got tired of having nothing and letting the devil cause her to worry! Based upon the words of Jesus, she wasn't going to be poor for very long.

> But he shall receive an hundredfold now in this time, houses, and brethren, and sisters, and mothers, and children, and lands, with persecutions; and in the world to come eternal life.
>
> —Mark 10:30

We get the idea that God wants 10 percent of our money. He doesn't want 10 percent of your money; He wants *all* of your money! He owns it; He's simply trusting you to handle it properly. When He says to give it and you in turn obey, you get positioned to step up to the concierge level of radical riches. Otherwise, you stay on the lower levels. But when you obey God in financial matters, all that you set your hand to, He'll bless. Every business you set out to build, everything you plan, He'll bless. I've found that when I do things on my own, those things are not blessed. It's hard work. By tithing and giving, you can actually put your finances on fast-forward. His blessings grease the way to quicker success.

REAL ESTATE

Deuteronomy 28:8 says, "He will bless thee in the land which the Lord gives thee."

My dear friend, Ken Gaub, told me about an older couple in his church who gave something in every offering. It didn't matter if it was Sunday morning, Sunday night, Wednesday night, or whenever there was an offering, they gave. They weren't rich. They didn't even know how they could afford to retire. They owned a little piece of farm property no one wanted-ed. It was narrow and long. They had cows, sold beef, churned butter, and grew vegetables.

One day the state highway department came along and wanted to put in a highway. The department had a choice: they could buy 30 different properties from other land own-ers, or they could turn the highway a little bit, make a curve in the road, and get it to run on that one thin, long piece of property. So they came to the elderly couple and offered them $3 million for the prop-erty.

"Your past isn't going to determine your future... unless you allow it to."

The couple accepted the money, had their house moved to another property and wrote out a $1 million check to their church. Then they got their old car repainted. She bought a pair of shoes. Then they figured they didn't need $2 million (which had come tax-free), so they gave another million to the church. Now they're living off the million dollars, at 10 percent interest a year. They're the happiest people you can imagine.

God can make your property enormously valuable when you learn that He owns everything. When He tells you to give, it's because He's trying to get you up to a higher level, the concierge level, *The Wealthy Place*. My retirement account doesn't belong to me — it belongs to God. My bank account doesn't belong to me — it belongs to God. But every time I obey and let go of something in my hand, God has something big in His hand he wants to give me.

Next I want to share some real-life examples of people who obeyed and prospered, or disobeyed and suffered the consequences.

When you tithe and give
offerings, you won't have
to do a lot of rebuking
because God will do it.

11
CHAPTER

OBEDIENCE
IN ACTION

I am an ordained Assemblies of God minister and a leader in the Michigan District of the Assemblies of God.

Presbyters call me frequently asking if I know of any pastors who can take churches that need a pastor. We have twenty-three churches in Michigan without pastors. One is a beautiful church with 70 members and a very nice parsonage. They can pay the pastor about $20,000 a year, but pastoral candidates keep turning it down. The last candidate sat in the interview, and his wife asked the deacons where the shopping mall was. They told her there was no mall nearby. She huffed, "Well then, it's not God's will for us to come here."

I can guarantee that pastor and his wife will never come into *The Wealthy Place* until they come out of disobedience! Money is *never* the bottom line. If money is your bottom line, you serve mammon. And you *cannot* serve both God and mammon.

No man can serve two masters: for either he will hate the one, and love the other; or else he will hold to the one, and despise the other. Ye cannot serve God and mammon.

—Matthew 6:24

FROM NOTHING TO WEALTH

A young evangelist went through a terrible divorce. His wife just couldn't put up with the demands of the ministry. The stress and the strain were too hard. She didn't want to pay the price, so she left him and took every material thing they had! He *felt* as if God could never use him again. All he could do was sit at his piano and write songs in his apartment, with bed sheets tacked up on the windows because he couldn't afford curtains. He didn't know what God was going to do with his life, if anything.

He thought he should try to find a job. First he sent some of his worship songs to a publisher, and the publisher liked them. They bought the songs and said they'd give him royalties when the songs were recorded.

Money is never the bottom line. If money is your bottom line, you serve mammon.

While he was praying one day, God spoke to him and said, "Your past isn't going to determine your future unless you allow it to." So he started making himself available again to speak in churches and other venues.

One local television ministry invited him to help with their telethon. Before he went, he checked his mail and there was a check for $5,000 from the music publisher! He thought, "I can get curtains!" He planned what he was going to do with the money, but during the telethon, as he spoke about planting seeds, the voice of the Lord came to him and said, "Give $1,000 to this ministry." For 45 minutes he argued with the Lord about whether he should get curtains or give $1,000. He didn't even have an oven in his studio apartment. The Lord didn't argue with him. He just gently insisted, "You either put me first, or you don't. It's that simple." Finally, the young evangelist wrote a check for $1,000 and gave it to the ministry.

The next Sunday morning, he got another preaching invitation. He was about to be introduced, but first the pastor was preparing to receive the offering. Just before the offering, the Lord spoke to him again and said, "Give $1,000 to this church." He responded, "Lord, I've only got $4,000 to my name!"

The Lord said, "You either put me first or you don't. It's that simple." So he wrote out a check for $1,000 and gave it to the church in the offering. He preached powerfully. That Sunday evening he was preaching in another little church. Just before the offering the Lord said, "Put $1,000 in the offering."

You either put God first, or you don't. It's that simple.

He whined, "Lord, you gave me $5,000 dollars and now you're making me give it all away. The Lord said, "No. I'm just teaching you to put me first in everything." Just before he gave the $1,000, God spoke a word to him and said, "When I speak

113

to you about planting a seed, it's because I have a harvest in mind for you."

So he wrote out another check for $1,000 and put it in the offering. He preached and at the end of the service a man walked up to him and showed him a catalogue of restored antique cars. He said, "You see that model right there? There were only 19 of them built in the world. They were handmade, and I have the one with serial number "one." During the service tonight, God told me to give it to you."

So he signed the title over, and suddenly the young evangelist owned this multi-thousand dollar car that was in beautiful condition. The next morning there was a knock at his door and a man standing at the door announced, "Brother, I heard you need a van for your ministry. I can't get this out of my mind. Go out and pick out any van you want, and I'll pay for it."

The next Tuesday, a guy called the young evangelist and said, "Brother, I need to meet you for lunch. It's an emergency." So he arranged to meet this man for lunch. The man was tired and worn out and said, "I haven't slept all night long. I've been wrestling with God. Last night when I laid my head down, God told me to give you $10,000. I couldn't sleep. Every time I'd try to sleep I'd hear that voice say, 'Give that young man $10,000.' I can't get any rest. Take this $10,000 so I can get some peace." And he handed $10,000 to the young evangelist across the lunch table.

That's how *The Wealthy Place* works. When you put God first in your life by coming into the place of obedience, you find God taking care of you in the most mysterious ways.

The Devourer Gone!

God said, "I will rebuke the devourer for your sakes." When you tithe and give offerings, you won't have to do a lot of rebuking because God will do it. Your tires may get 80,000 miles instead of 40,000. Your refrigerator will not break down every other week. Your shoes will last longer. You'll find great deals at the store.

Let me tell you about Louise, a 50-year-old divorcee. She believes in giving a little to charity once in a while but not in tithing. Bad things are always happening to Louise, but she doesn't seem to connect it to her disobedience. She already has one of those consolidated loans to pay off all her debts and credit cards. Then, one day she realizes her roof is leaking. It's going to cost $6,000 to fix the roof. But she has a relative who will do it for $2,000, so she's excited. He takes off the tiles and finds the wood is rotting. It's going to cost a little more. He tears off the roof, and there's no rain in the forecast, so he doesn't cover it up for the night. That night it rains in the house. The walls are all ruined, the floor is ruined, the linoleum peels up.

She hires someone to clean it up and someone to repaint. This $6,000 job she was going to get for $2,000 ends up being a $16,000 expense. She doesn't believe in tithing, so the devourer isn't rebuked from her life.

I've known many people like Louise. I remember Dan and Mary, real people, standing up in a church service weeping their eyes out, crying, "We need to apologize to this congregation and beg forgiveness. We haven't been here on Sunday nights; we haven't been here on Wednesday nights. We haven't been tithing because we've been building our retirement home up at the lake. We went up there to work last Sunday afternoon and found our house and everything in it, including all of our picture albums, in a pile of ash. It had burned down, and we had no insurance. Everything was lost. We will never again withhold the tithe that belongs to the Lord."

The devourer must be rebuked by God Himself if you're going to get out of the mediocre place and into *The Wealthy Place.*

TITHING ISN'T OPTIONAL

If you give less than 10 percent of your gross income to the Lord, you are not tithing.

A man told me he was "tithing" to his son who was in college and needed the help. The guy's business then went belly-up. He didn't understand why. Well, it's really quite simple. It's because the devourer wasn't rebuked! The tithe isn't to go to your son in college. That option, biblically, isn't available. The tithe goes to the storehouse, the church treasury. Always!

At Mount Hope Church we have a tithe guarantee. I tell people that if they bring 10 percent of their gross income for 12 months and they're not better off financially at the end of that 12 months, to bring their check stubs, W2 forms, and tax returns to our office (so we can verify that they tithed 10 percent of their gross income), and we will give the whole tithe back. I've had people test me on this.

Recently a lady demanded, "I want my tithe back. I'm worse off financially." I said, "Okay, bring in your check stubs." She sputtered a bit and whined, "I've never been able to give the *full* tithe." Listen to me. There is no such thing as a "half tithe." There is no provision in God's Word for a half tithe, quarter tithe, eighth tithe or a tenth tithe. The tithe is 10 percent of your gross income. If you're not tithing, you are simply in disobedience. And to come into *The Wealthy Place* you must first come out of disobedience.

Some women have husbands who won't let them tithe. If you're working and you have a paycheck, your husband cannot force you to disobey God with the tithe. If it's his paycheck and he doesn't want to tithe, you're stuck and you're going to stay in the place of mediocrity with him all your life. You will never get into *The Wealthy Place*, and I feel sorry for you. If I were you, I'd pray that your husband would come to Jesus Christ in true salvation, be baptized in water, be baptized in the Holy Ghost, and get a revelation of what Jesus really did for us on the Cross. Then you're going to have a new man and he'll be a tither!

Anyone who doesn't tithe cannot truly have an intimate relationship with Jesus Christ.

Listen you dads, you heads of the households. You have an immense responsibility on your shoulders. You will answer to God for your obedience or disobedience, as the case may be. Do not neglect the tithe! It's the first step toward coming out of disobedience. It's not difficult to do. Just write the check, put it in the offering plate. There's nothing hard about it. It's just a matter of doing it. Put God to the test. He said this is the one area where you can test Him.

Take that step out of disobedience so you can step into much more wealth than you've ever had in your life.

Now let's move to the second letter in the D-I-D acronym, the "I."

I*t's not how much income*
you earn but what you do with
that income that determines
your level of wealth.

CHAPTER 12

COMING OUT OF "IGNORANCE"

The first "D" of the D-I-D acronym stands for coming out of disobedience.

THE "I":
COMING OUT OF "IGNORANCE"

I interview pastors as part of my responsibilities to the Michigan district of my denomination. In a recent meeting, one candidate came before the executive committee and said he wanted to plant a church. I asked him what books he'd read about church planting in the last six months. He said he hadn't read any and couldn't afford to buy books.

I voted "no" on his assignment. Why? Because to be deliberately ignorant about something that God has called you to do is a high spiritual crime, in my opinion.

I meet people who say they can't afford books and tapes, but they'll eat at the Outback restaurant and think nothing of paying a $36 check. They'll go with six people to Burger King and spend $19.95, but do you think they'll buy a book? They complain that books cost too much! Yet they get that restaurant bill, sign the credit card, and don't think a thing of it.

GOING AFTER KNOWLEDGE

Anything that helps get you out of the place of mediocrity and into *The Wealthy Place* is worth it! To come out of ignorance, you need to make an investment in personal knowledge.

There are two kinds of knowledge: spiritual and practical. Spiritual knowledge we get from God's Word. Practical knowledge we get from qualified people who have experience in certain areas.

For example, back in 1993 when I needed to learn how to fly a Cessna aircraft, I needed practical knowledge. The Bible is not an aviation manual. I needed a qualified instructor to teach me how to fly.

Here's another example. When I first became a pastor, I was a "green bean." I'd never been a pastor before in my life. I had all kinds of people, including pastors, giving me advice, but I looked at their lives or their ministries and asked myself if I wanted to be like them. If I didn't, I didn't take their advice. I only listened to qualified, successful advisors.

Several years ago I paid Joe Gandolfo $1,000. Dr. Gandolfo is perhaps one of the richest men in America and a very devoted Christian. He lives in Lakeland, Florida, and advises many famous and successful people. I wanted to sit with him for a morning and learn everything I could. Mary Jo and I went down to Lakeland and spent the morning with Joe — this legend, this money magnet.

Anything that helps get you out of the place of mediocrity and into The Wealthy Place is worth it!

Joe is a generous soul. He'll drive through town and find where an elderly widow lives who needs a new roof on her house, and he'll personally pay a roofing company to do it. He gives way beyond a tithe.

Mary Jo and I listened to Joe intently as he shared with us. I took him copies of all my account balances and said, "Joe, I need some knowledge. I need to know how to make better investments and get my financial life in order." He gave me some advice, and I took notes. It was like sitting at the feet of a giant. Maybe you've seen him on the 700 Club. He looks great at 70 years old, but you'd think he's only 39 or 40. When you see him sitting in his office you'll notice how casual and comfortable he is. He'll wear sweatpants and T-shirt on a typical day.

Money doesn't like hanging around with ignorance or incompetence.

He built a chapel in his office building and spends an hour a day praying there because he knows that the key to wealth is seeking first the Kingdom of God. He showed us his private workout room where he walks on the treadmill while watching the 700 Club on a big-screen television. He took me to another room with a big, bubbly hot tub he uses to relax and think.

He told me about real estate and put me in touch with a few other people who were experts in real estate who could help me. We determined at that time what my net worth was. If I died, that's all they could get out of my accounts. It wasn't much for a 40-some-year-old person. I now believe that by the time you're between 40 and 50 you ought to have at least $1 million in your wealth accounts if you're following God's principles.

Seven years after that morning with Joe, I realized my net assets had multiplied more than 12 times. Was that original $1,000 I paid to Joe Gandolfo an expense? Of course not. It was an investment. I'd never trade back that $1,000 for the wealth I enjoy now. Are tapes and books an expense? No. They're an investment in your future.

I bought my kids the book, *Rich Dad, Poor Dad.* I think every believer ought to read that book. I bought it while I was vacationing in Florida just before I launched my island real estate venture. It was like the windows of knowledge opened up to me. I couldn't put the book down. I went out and bought 20 copies of the book and gave a copy to Trina and David, my children. I gave a copy to my staff too. I suggest you read it and get motivated.

Start learning and thinking about *The Wealthy Place*. I bought my kids the *Debt Free and Prosperous Living Course* by John Cummuta, a four-tape series that cost me $89 for each set. I want them thinking in terms of debt-free and prosperous living. I want my son and daughter to have at least $2-3 million in assets before they're 40.

You have to learn the "nuts and bolts" of wealth from people who have been there.

WHAT IS WEALTH TO YOU?

I sometimes ask people to define wealth. They usually say something like this, "If I was making $1,000 a week, I'd be wealthy." But that's not wealth! That's income. I'm talking about real wealth. Hard assets.

I sometimes ask people what they want 10 years from now, and 99 percent of them can't tell me. They have no clue. Therefore, they'll, have to take whatever life gives them. Mark 11:24 says:

Learn the "nuts and bolts" of wealth from people who have been there.

> Therefore I say unto you, What things soever ye desire, when ye pray, believe that ye receive them, and ye shall have them.

Things are objects or objectives. If you don't know what you want, you can't even pray right! You must know what you want if you are going to move into *The Wealthy Place*.

At one time it was hard to believe that pastors could be millionaires, and yet I'm seeing it more and more. Even missionaries are telling me that these principles have revolutionized their lives. Most missionaries take 18 months to raise their support. But one missionary told me he used the principles he learned in my book *Radical Riches*, and as a result raised all of his support in just 10 months. He's on the mission field right now. Why? Because the wealth principles work. Remember, you have to come out of disobedience first and out of ignorance next.

Your salary does not equal your wealth!

Theodore Johnson worked as an employee for United Parcel Service. He was just a common man, but he came out of the mediocre place and into *The Wealthy Place*. Today he is worth a cool $70 million. Understand this: your salary does not equal your wealth!

I received a letter from a man who said he didn't see how these principles could work for him with the job he had. He was looking to his paycheck as his source instead of to God, and that's an attitude problem. Your paycheck does not determine your wealth.

When you are looking to the wrong place as your source, you're going to be disappointed every time.

INCOME IS NOT WEALTH

Your income has nothing to do with your wealth. This may shock you. I know a pastor who never made more than $12,500 a year all of his life. He retired a few years ago as a millionaire. It's not how much income you earn but what you do with that income that will determine your future wealth.

Many people make the basic mistake of thinking they need to increase their income in order to increase their wealth. So they get a second job. Or pester their boss for a pay raise. Or respond to one of those ads that promise you can "make $2,000 a week in your spare time." It becomes a game of trying to pump up the income. That is *not* the way into *The Wealthy Place!*

Those living in the mediocre place keep looking at *The Wealthy Place* thinking, "Why can't I get over there? I'm going to the pep rallies; I'm selling Apple Brand Fiber Tablets in my spare time." They don't seem

When you are looking to the wrong place as your source, you're going to be disappointed every time.

to understand, you have to come out of one place before you can get into another place. It's the law of physics. If I want to go to Detroit, I have to come out of Lansing and point my car in the direction of Detroit. If you want to come into *The Wealthy Place*, you have to come out of the room of disobedience and ignorance. You have to come out of "the mediocre room" to get into *The Wealthy Place*.

Money doesn't like hanging around with ignorance or incompetence.

Come out of ignorance! Agree with the Scriptures. Get knowledge from people who know more than you. Invest money on gaining knowledge, not on get-rich-quick schemes.

There's one more "D" in the D-I-D acronym. It may be the biggest "D" that keeps people from moving into *The Wealthy Place*.

The debt mentality is so ingrained in the American mindset that people consider it normal.

CHAPTER 13

COME OUT OF "DEBT!"

Here's the last "D" in the D-I-D acronym: Debt. Debt is the single biggest trap that is keeping people out of *The Wealthy Place* today. Refinancing with low monthly payments can be a trap. Credit cards that carry a balance are a trap. You think you're doing well because you have a 6 percent interest loan on your house, but you're still giving away hundreds of thousands of dollars more than the original cost of the home. Debt can gobble away 75 percent of your wealth...or more.

Ninety-six percent of the people in America will never enjoy more than 25 percent of what they earn in their lifetime because of debt. A person making $50,000 a year often has less than $14,000 for tithes, offerings, clothes, vacations, college, and utility bills because of debt. They wonder why they're not making enough money.

The debt mentality is so ingrained in the American mind-set that people consider it normal. The little tenants rise up in your mind and say, "I can't afford to pay cash." If you can't afford to pay cash, you can't afford it — period.

In the 1970s when property values were appreciating at 25 percent a year, it may have made sense to get an 8 percent loan for the short term. But today debt is a way of life. Companies in Japan now offer 50 year mortgages. In America they're now beginning to introduce 40 year mortgages.

WE WANT IT NOW

People dream about having a new kitchen, and they're willing to go into debt over it. Instead they should go down to Home Depot, throw a can of paint on that kitchen, and let it hold them over until they have the cash to pay for a remodel job. You don't need a new kitchen with oak cabinets if you can't pay cash for it. Wait until you come into *The Wealthy Place*, and you can buy a whole oak house if you want.

You should treat a mortgage as you would an unwelcome guest and plan to get rid of it as quickly as possible.

Do you know what the real problem is? People don't want to wait.

An experiment was once done with little children. They were placed in a room with a one-way mirror so researchers could observe them. They told the kids they could play with all the toys in the room, but there was a bag of marshmallows on the table that they were told not to touch. If the children ate even one, they wouldn't get any more; but if they resisted the temptation and didn't eat any, they would get a whole bag of marshmallows at the end of the session. As soon as the adults left, the kids ig-

Debt is the single biggest trap that is keeping people out of The Wealthy Place today.

nored the toys and stared at those marshmallows. They tried to resist. You could almost see their minds working.

It's the same way banks and retailers work, offering low monthly payments or no payments until June and all that. They want you to eat one "marshmallow" now and sacrifice your whole bag.

Most of the kids that day ate a marshmallow. A couple of little girls held off. The researcher came in the room and gave the girls who resisted a whole bag, and the others none. The kids who ate the marshmallows all cried, "That's not fair!" But it was very fair. Those who followed the rules were rewarded.

Adults do the same thing. We want everything now, so we take a "marshmallow" and sell out our wealth for the future and then wonder why we can't get into that door leading to *The Wealthy Place.*

STRANGLED BY DEBT

I talked with a young couple that couldn't afford anything and could hardly make ends meet. We figured they were spending $200 a month on pizza, video rentals, fast food, cappuccinos and lattes. It's amazing how fast food can add up. You don't think it's much — only $7 for a meal, or $2.30 for a premium cup of coffee. But we figured that if they paid that extra $200 on their mortgage, it would lower the payoff time from 30 years to 17 years, saving them $156,000 in wealth! All they had to do was deny the pizza, deny the video rentals, and deny the fast food.

Another real couple had a $1,000-a-month mortgage at 7 percent and they figured that they could make an extra $1,000 a month house payment. So they're paying $2,000 a month on their $1,000 a month house payment. They're bringing the debt down from 30 years to 8 years. They're saving *$264,000 of their wealth!* You have to be willing to come out of *this* place (debt) in order to get into *that* place (*The Wealthy Place*).

If you are eating your marshmallows now, don't say it's not fair when other people who have denied themselves start walking into *The Wealthy Place* while you're still in the mediocre place. If you are faithful over a little, Jesus said He would give you charge over much (Matthew 25:41). Listen! You're *not* being faithful over a little if you're giving away hundreds of thousands of dollars of personal wealth to interest payments to credit institutions. That's money the Lord put *you* in charge of. It goes down the black hole of interest. Wouldn't you rather have that money working for you instead of against you?

Here's an example of mismanagement. If you typically buy airline tickets at the last minute, which cost $300 dollars more than if you had planned ahead and purchased them two weeks earlier, are you being a faithful manager of the Lord's money?

Let's look at a third couple that has a $1,000-a-month mortgage. They don't pay any more on the mortgage because they enjoy the tax deduction. They deduct $6,000 in interest on their taxes every year, thinking that's a good deal. They could give that same amount to the Lord's work and get the same tax deduction, but they don't consider that! If you are in the 28 percent tax bracket, that deduction is like giving a dollar to taxes and getting 28 cents back in return. What kind of "deal" is that? I wouldn't mind making that kind of money! You give me a dollar and I give you 28 cents? Sure! I'll take that deal. In reality, a tax deduction may be a nice thing, but it is not an asset.

Deducting mortgage interest isn't a great deduction at all. You're still paying 72 cents or more on each dollar of interest, and you could be giving it to the Lord and investing for your future.

THE DEATH GRIP

The word "mortgage" comes from the same root word as mortician, and it means death grip. It's a trap.

It's okay to borrow on an appreciating asset if you can pay it off quickly. If you put $8,000 a year in interest payments, you better be sure your investment is appreciating by at least that much.

A rule of thumb is to pay your mortgage in seven years or less when you buy a property and make sure you can make double payments on it.

If you can't make at least double payments on it, it's a property you probably can't afford. There are rare exceptions. For example, one exception would be when you get an excellent deal and can raise the value of the property in a short time with some "elbow grease" and "sweat equity."

One time, I borrowed some money for a $180,000 property. My wife and I invested three weeks working on it, and brought the value up to $259,000, with $14,000 in expenses. So in three weeks we had:

$180,000 in property costs
$14,000 in fix up costs
$3,000 in closing cost and interest
$197,000 total expenses
_____

$ 259,000 New Value

That equals $62,000 profit in 3 weeks. In cases like this, it makes sense to borrow. We now rent the property at $1,800 a month, which more than covers the expenses to operate, and the total property value continues to appreciate.

But normally you should treat a mortgage as you would an unwelcome guest and plan to get rid of it as quickly as possible.

GET EMPLOYEES

To come into *The Wealthy Place*, money has to become your employee. I have employees right now working for me. I work 10 or 12 hours a day, 60 to 80 hours a week. I love every minute of it. I love being a pastor. I love teaching, going verse by verse through the Bible. But I have employees outside of the ministry working for me. They're called dollars, and they live in the mutual funds, stocks, and rental real estate I own.

When you own stocks, you're an owner. When you buy bonds, you're a loaner. We, as covenant people, are supposed to be the owners and the loaners. That means we're supposed to have stocks, bonds, and properties. Stocks are like little employees out there working for you. They're out there getting other employees and adding them to your accounts. I don't even have to watch over them very much. I just let them go to work. But I have to give them the right environment in which to work.

I made a fortune in power company stock when it dropped from $50 a share to $16 a share just because of a small dividend cut. It was a good company, so when its price dropped I called my employees and put them to work to get another fortune. The stock soon went up to $37 a share. Already I had earned 21 more "employees" per share. That's one way of making your money work for you instead of against you.

When you are earning interest (yield, growth, or value appreciation), the money is working for you. When you are *paying* interest, money is working against you.

Stop and think for a moment. Who would you trust with your money? Someone who is making you more money or someone who is throwing your money into a whirling black hole? Well, that's the way God sees it. Remember the story we looked at in chapter one of the master who entrusted his servants with his money while he was on a trip? Let's revisit this story from The Living Bible.

> The Kingdom of Heaven can be illustrated by the story of a man going into another country, who called together his servants and loaned them money to invest for him while he was gone. "He gave $5,000 to one, $2,000 to another, and $1,000 to the last—dividing it in proportion to their abilities—and then left on his trip.

> The man who received the $5,000 began immediately to buy and sell with it and soon earned another $5,000.

> The man with $2,000 went right to work, too, and earned another $2,000.

> "But the man who received the $1,000 dug a hole in the ground and hid the money for safekeeping.

> "After a long time their master returned from his trip and called them to him to account for his money.

> The man to whom he had entrusted the $5,000 brought him $10,000.

> "His master praised him for good work. 'You have been faithful in handling this small amount,' he told him, 'so now I will give you many more responsibilities. Begin the joyous tasks I have assigned to you.'

> "Next came the man who had received the $2,000, with the report, 'Sir, you gave me $2,000 to use, and I have doubled it.'

> " 'Good work,' his master said. 'You are a good and faithful servant. You have been faithful over this small amount, so now I will give you much more.'

"Then the man with the $1,000 came and said, 'Sir, I knew you were a hard man, and I was afraid you would rob me of what I earned, so I hid your money in the earth and here it is!'

"But his master replied, 'Wicked man! Lazy slave! Since you knew I would demand your profit, you should at least have put my money into the bank so I could have some interest.

Take the money from this man and give it to the man with the $10,000.

For the man who uses well what he is given shall be given more, and he shall have abundance. But from the man who is unfaithful, even what little responsibility he has shall be taken from him.

And throw the useless servant out into outer darkness: there shall be weeping and gnashing of teeth.'

—Matthew 25:15-30 (TLB)

When God sees your faith and your obedience, He's going to bring you into *The Wealthy Place*. Psalm 118:23 and 25 talks about how fast He brought the children of Israel into *The Wealthy Place*. They were in slavery to Egypt, but Moses was persistent. "Let my people go, let them go." He persisted, and the people of God kept seeking God, crying out to Him. Finally the people of the world (Egypt) got so fed up they said, "Here, take our silver, take our gold, take our valuables, and get out."

When we come out of disobedience, ignorance and debt (D-I-D), marvelous things begin to happen. If we try to get into *The Wealthy Place* our own way, looking for a second job, trying to scrape money over from *The Wealthy Place* without coming into *The Wealthy Place*, we get disappointed. I'd rather let God put me into *The Wealthy Place*. I'd rather have the windows of Heaven open, so wisdom, anointing and favor is pouring into my life! I would rather have God's wealth pursuing me than me chasing after rainbows.

This subject of coming out of debt is so important, I want to devote another chapter to it, to help you get free!

G*oing heavily into debt*
for the sake of present gratification
is disobedience.

14

CHAPTER

TAKE THE STEP
TO FREEDOM

Many Christians live the same way as non-Christians: in debt up to their ears. Most people pay $6,000-8,000 a year in interest payments on houses, cars, stereos, tape-of-the-month clubs and credit cards. That's money you can't give to God or use for yourself and your family. And people wonder why they can't make ends meet.

Consumer debt has the potential of bringing 120 different curses on your life. In the Old Testament you'll find 120 different curses that can come as a result of disobedience. And going heavily into debt for the sake of present gratification *is* disobedience. The devil will devour your wealth through debt. Most people in America will earn between $2-3 million in the course of their lifetime, but much of that bleeds away in interest. People say the boss isn't paying them enough. They say, "I'm planting seeds but I'm not getting my harvest." You're getting your harvest but you're giving it to the bank and the credit industry. One dollar of debt right now can cost you over $600 in future wealth. $6,000 in annual interest payments has the potential of costing you $3.6 million in future wealth.

HARD MATH

Why is it that God doesn't seem to be exalting more of His people? It's because God resists the proud and exalts the humble.

> ...God resisteth the proud, and giveth grace to the humble.
>
> —1 Peter 5:5c

> A man's pride shall bring him low: but honour shall uphold the humble in spirit.
>
> —Proverbs 29:23

It's humiliating to buy a $60,000 house that needs fixing up when all your friends live in $300,000 homes. It's humiliating to drive an old car when you can borrow the money and get a new car and smile and wave like a proud papa.

I had to change my thoughts, my attitudes, my mental "tenants" to get on the wealthy side with God.

I talked recently with a young married couple who had a brand-new baby...and $27,000 on their credit cards. They just bought a house and have a $65,000 mortgage on a two-bedroom, 100 year-old house. If they never charge another thing on their credit card and make the minimum payment, it will take them *thirty years* to pay off their credit card. It will cost them $151,000 to pay off that $27,000 credit card debt alone! That's $151,000 of their wealth gone because of debt.

I know another lady who has $38,000 of credit card debt.

You say your credit card is only charging 8 percent. That's fine if you're paying it off every month and not actually paying that interest. But if you don't pay it off and you run a balance, you pay interest on interest on interest. For example, if you make the minimum payment one month, you pay interest not only on the balance, but also on the interest that has accrued against you. If you continue to accumulate consumer debt (buying anything that depreciates in value) you're doomed. You'll never get to *The Wealthy Place*. There isn't a thing God or I can do for you.

In Deuteronomy 28:12 it clearly says, "...thou shalt lend unto many nations, and thou shalt not borrow." He promises that if you obey this, He'll make you the head and not the tail. But the vast majority of American people are the tail. Less than 4 percent are in the top of the financial pyramid, on the concierge level. Those on the first level are doomed to stay there unless they understand that consumer debt is the devourer taking the lion's share of their wealth.

Consumer debt has the potential of bringing 120 different curses on your life.

Buying a car is the same thing. General Motors employees get a discount on new cars and think they "scored" with a 4 percent loan. Listen! It's insane to borrow money for a new car. I don't care if you're paying 1 percent on the loan. The minute you hop into that car and pull onto the street, it loses 15-25 percent of its value. Now you're paying a loan on value that's no longer there! Do you think God will trust you with wealth if that's your thinking?

The Bible makes provision for short-term, low-interest loans. But you must make sure it's short-term and that you're borrowing on an appreciating asset such as property or buildings. Then set a concrete goal to have it paid off in five to seven years.

WHAT HOUSES REALLY COST

As a lender or an owner, your money is constantly working for you. As a borrower, it's constantly working against you. You have to decide which you'll be. Imagine that you get a $125,000 mortgage. Your payment is $1,000, but most of it is interest. Maybe $950 of your first payment will go to interest and only $50 to principal. Now they add interest to the balance and you're paying on that too. You're stuck in this cycle of paying the highest interest in the first seven years of a thirty-year loan and very little toward getting your principal balance down. That's why I encourage people to pay extra on the principal balance every month.

Wealth flows to humble people, not the arrogant.

You have to consider, too, what you're losing by not investing your money elsewhere. Say you have a credit card, and it's costing you only 8 percent. But you could be earning 12 percent in an index fund, so effectively it's as if you're paying 20 percent interest. That's called opportunity cost — the cost of lost opportunities.

Or say you take out an $80,000 mortgage at 8 percent interest on a 30-year loan. Your total cost is actually $211,327. That's what the house will really cost you. Of course, the bank is more than willing to help. They'll advertise that they're customer oriented, relationship builders. They'll give you a home equity loan so you can make home improvements. You think you have the greatest bank in the world, and all the while the devourer is stealing, killing, and destroying your wealth.

You probably have personal experience with the whirling black hole of debt. Think of people who owe their future paychecks to new cars, stereos, furniture, and credit cards. The devil advertises low monthly payments, and people snatch them up.

$6,000 in annual interest payments has the potential of costing you $3.6 million in future wealth.

The main reason people go into debt is they are not humble enough to drive a used car or do without life's luxuries for a season. I personally buy cars that are two or three years old, after someone else has taken the 25 percent hit on depreciation. I pay cash for them rather than paying a bank a couple thousand dollars extra to give me a loan. I don't want my future wealth to be destroyed. I Peter 5:6 says if you humble yourself, God will exalt you in due season. But if you try to exalt yourself before God does, you get *humbled* in due season.

...thou shalt lend unto many nations, and thou shalt not borrow.

There is an "exclusive" city in Michigan where many of the homes are valued at $600,000 to $6,000,000. The people drive BMWs and Mercedes. But guess which city in Michigan has the highest level of foreclosures and bankruptcies? Yes! The same city. People won't humble themselves now for the sake of their future wealth, and as a result, they get humbled.

WHY WEALTH GOES TO THE WEALTHY

For unto every one that hath shall be given, and he shall have abundance: but from him that hath not shall be taken away even that which he hath.

—Matthew 25:29

Some people get upset because the Master gave more to those who already had plenty.

People complain, "The rich are getting richer and the poor are getting poorer."

Those socialist-like words are spoken from a poverty mentality. If the rich are getting richer, why not just move over to the rich side instead of complaining about it? You decide. Deuteronomy 30:19 says you can choose blessing or curses.

> I call heaven and earth to record this day against you, that I have set before you life and death, blessing and cursing: therefore choose life, that both thou and thy seed may live.
>
> —Deuteronomy 30:19

Choose the blessing! Choose the blessing of having wealth to lend to nations. That's how God's people ought to operate. I want to have the wealth to lend to nations. I want to have some nation say, "Pastor Williams, will you loan me $10 million? Or how about $10 billion?"

Jesus said in Luke 16, if you can't be trusted with worldly wealth, who is going to trust you with true riches?

> If therefore ye have not been faithful in the unrighteous mammon, who will commit to your trust the true riches?
>
> —Luke 16:11

> And if you are untrustworthy about worldly wealth, who will trust you with the true riches of heaven?
>
> —Luke 16:11 (TLB)

If you don't handle what He's entrusted to you properly now, He's going to take it from you and give it to the one who *is* handling it properly and making it grow. This idea used to anger me, but it's God's book, not mine. I had to change my thoughts, my attitudes, my mental "tenants," to get on the wealthy side with God.

If the rich are getting richer, why not just move over to the rich side instead of complaining about it? You decide.

I now see that my wealth isn't tied to stock market crashes or recessions. It's tied to the favor of God, and to my own ability to handle money well by using biblical principles. If a depression comes, people in *The Wealthy Place* will have the greatest opportunities. But those who refused to come out of debt will struggle just to make their interest payments.

Thou hast caused men to ride over our heads; we went through fire and through water: but thou broughtest us out into a wealthy place.

—Psalm 66:12

Notice the terminology used. "We went through the fire and we went through the water." We use these terms today.

"Money burns a hole in my pocket."

"My mailbox was flooded with bills today."

"I'm practically drowning in this debt."

"I can't keep my head above water financially."

You hear people use those terms all the time, don't you? Perhaps you are going through the fire and flood. You feel ensnared, trapped. How do you get out?

Believers are supposed to be the lenders and the owners,

not the borrowers and the debtors. Many Christians are going through the fire and the flood because of disobedience. We have become so much like the world in our financial thinking. Believers are supposed to be different. We watch the same television programs everyone else watches. We hear the Ditech.com commercials, and we get on

Wealth isn't tied to stock market crashes or recessions. It's tied to the favor of God.

our computers to apply for a second mortgage. We get caught up in the thinking of this world. But unless you come out of debt, it will steal from you every bit of wealth God intended for you.

As I mentioned previously, there are some situations where you could borrow at a low interest rate for an opportunity with appreciating value. But in most cases, let's view debt-free living as a commandment. Thou shalt not kill. Thou shalt not steal. Thou shalt not commit adultery. Thou shalt not borrow.

You say, "Dave, it's only an 8 percent loan." Okay, using that logic, you'd have to say, "Thou shalt not commit adultery except for 8 percent of the time" or, "Thou shalt not kill except for 8 percent of the time." "Thou shalt not bear false witness except 8 percent of the time." Isn't it the same kind of logic? Okay, I may be a tad extreme here, but I think you get the point.

Next I've condensed the wealth principles into a checklist you can use to remind yourself of the right steps toward *The Wealthy Place*.

*C*ertain attitudes attract wealth.
Certain attitudes repel wealth.

15

CHAPTER

CHECKLIST
FOR WEALTH

The Wealthy Place is the right place to be. I've been in the other room. I like the wealthy room better.

Here are some action steps that will help to take you out of the mediocre place and bring you into *The Wealthy Place*.

❑ **NUMBER ONE: ACCEPT RESPONSIBILITY FOR YOUR FINANCIAL CONDITION.**

Every one of us is responsible for where we are financially. If somebody says, "My ex-husband got me in this mess," or "The economy wrecked my portfolio," they are moving down the path of poverty. No matter what has happened to you or me, the starting point of wealth is taking responsibility for your present condition. Now.

❏ **NUMBER TWO: PREPARE TO MAKE AN INCREDIBLE COMMITMENT.**

When we have God-directed finances, He can tell us what to do with our money at any time, and we *must* obey. He may allow you to store up $250,000, and in a moment's notice, He could tell you to give it all to missions. But if He does, it's because He's preparing to entrust even more to you, and a great harvest is on the way.

I have found that when we are wise managers of His money, and when our hearts are in the right place, He allows us to manage larger and larger amounts, which requires larger commitment and larger sacrifice.

❏ **NUMBER THREE: PREPARE FOR SCRUTINY AND CRITICISM.**

Wealth brings with itself incredible pressure. People love to scrutinize those with wealth, as if the wealth came from the onlookers' personal pockets. I read about a minister who was criticized for his salary, but people didn't know he was giving eight times more from personal investments to missions than what the church was paying him. People felt it was their duty to criticize him because he was receiving a large salary. Things are not always as they seem.

❏ **NUMBER FOUR: PREPARE TO BE COURAGEOUS.**

Wealth requires risk. Every investment is risky. Without risk there is no reward. There will be setbacks, but don't let them deter you.

❏ **NUMBER FIVE: PLAN FOR WEALTH, NOT POVERTY.**

• Do you have a plan for wealth? Do you have a

balanced, biblical approach to allocating your assets?

- Do you know what you want to accomplish financially in the next five years? Ten years?

- Do you know what you want your finances to look like when you retire? Are you doing anything today to make that happen?

- Do you dream of what you could do with greater wealth?

Plan for wealth now, or you will end up without it.

WEALTH SWITCHES

Let me give you a set of switches that will activate the power to get wealth. These should be built into every Christian's life.

❏ SWITCH ONE: THE FEAR OF THE LORD.

> By humility and fear of the Lord are riches, honor and life.
>
> —Proverbs 22:4

> Riches profit not in the day of wrath: but righteousness delivereth from death.
>
> —Proverbs 11:4

The fear of the Lord has to be first, and that means to be born again and employing the principles found in God's Word — the Bible.

❏ SWITCH TWO: TRUE HUMILITY.

It's worth repeating Proverbs 22:4: "By humility and fear of the Lord are riches, honor and life."

Sometimes when wealth flows our way we have a tendency to become arrogant. But I have noticed that those who are the wealthiest — ones whom God seems to be blessing — have a humble spirit about them. I met a man 20 years ago who was a millionaire as a result of buying the exclusive rights to a toy "potato gun" that shoots small bits of potato. He was one of the most humble people I ever met. You could talk with him as you would talk with anyone else.

Wealth flows to humble people, not the arrogant.

❏ SWITCH THREE: ATTITUDES AND THOUGHTS.

Remember this. Proverbs 21:5a says, "The thoughts of the diligent tend only to plenteousness." Certain attitudes attract wealth. Certain attitudes repel wealth. Reread the chapter on attitudes and the poverty mentality and get your thinking in line.

❏ SWITCH FOUR: TEACHABILITY.

Poverty and shame shall be to him that refuseth instruction...

—Proverbs 13:18a

Eight out of 10 businesses fail within two years and that includes Christian businesses. I have asked people, "Did you study your field and learn from successful people who made it in that business?" and Christians have said, "No, I just figured God would bless me."

When I knew that God had called me to the ministry, I got books on preaching and teaching; being a successful pastor; growing your church; and how to minister to people better. I didn't want failure to result from my ignorance or lack of study.

❑ SWITCH FIVE: PLANNING.

My observation tells me that maybe 4 or 5 percent of people plan for wealth.

> We can make our plans, but the LORD determines our steps.
>
> —Proverbs 16:9 (NLT)

> The wise have wealth and luxury, but fools spend whatever they get.
>
> —Proverbs 21:20 (NLT)

Mary Jo and I taught our kids to put away ten percent of everything they get whether it's an allowance or birthday money. We taught them not only to give 10 percent to Jesus, but to save 10 percent. When they were little we even charged them 5 percent for taxes. (Actually we put that money in a bank account for them.) That taught them responsibility.

When I started in the ministry, I saved a little bit from my meager income, cashed in a 500 dollar insurance policy, and made some investments. It is tough to hold any money back when you live below the national poverty line. But after a year, the value of that investment was $1,000. I cashed it in and reinvested it in a mutual fund just in time for a rally in the market, and the money doubled, then tripled, then tripled again.

Planning gives you power in the long run.

❑ SWITCH SIX: HONESTY AND INTEGRITY.

Stay out of get-rich-quick schemes. Beware of "free wealth-building" seminars. Stay away from lotteries too. True wealth doesn't usually come overnight.

> Wealth from get-rich-quick schemes quickly disappears; wealth from hard work grows.
>
> —Proverbs 13:11 (NLT)

> ...the person who wants to get rich quick will only get into trouble.
>
> —Proverbs 28:20b

This is my main problem with lotteries. They cater to people's desire to get rich quick. Studies have shown that a large percentage of the people who win the lottery have nothing to show for it just three years later.

❑ SWITCH SEVEN: FAITH.

> Now faith is the substance of things hoped for, the evidence of things not seen.
>
> —Hebrews 11:1

Faith brings God into our financial affairs. When I made my first investment, I went through every prospectus with a magnifying glass to make sure the mutual fund didn't buy stocks from tobacco or liquor companies or drug companies that provided abortion drugs. I did that because I have faith in God more than in the stock market, and I aim to please Him. I think that's why He blessed my little investment so much.

I knew of a man who owned a gas station on a busy intersection. When he became a Christian he wanted to shut it down on Sundays and invite his workers to church, but there were three gas stations on the other corners competing with him. They scoffed, "If you close on Sunday, you will never make it in this business." By faith he did it anyway.

On Monday he opened up the gas station, and it happened that an Army caravan was coming through town. They pulled every single truck into his gas station, and he made enough money to match what he would have made on a Sunday. Not only that, every Monday thereafter the Army caravan stopped at his gas station and filled up their vehicles.

His faith flipped the switch!

❑ SWITCH EIGHT: PLANTING AND GIVING.

> It is possible to give freely and become more wealthy, but those who are stingy will lose everything.
>
> The generous prosper and are satisfied; those who refresh others will themselves be refreshed.
>
> —Proverbs 11:24-25 (NLT)

I like to observe how people tip waitresses because it tells me what their bank account will look like in the days to come. The liberal man shall be rich, and his own soul shall become fat.

Malachi 3:8-11 says to bring in the tithes and offerings into the storehouse. God will open the windows of Heaven, pour you out a blessing when you obey. Money is like a crop, and some of it must be used as "seed." If somebody gave you an ear of corn, you could eat the whole thing and have nothing left; you could plant some, eat the rest, and have corn in the coming years.

Money works that way. When we sow in generous giving, we plant seed. Isaiah 55:10-11 says God gives the seed, meaning everybody has something to plant. That means you! I constantly hear people make faith-destroying remarks, such as, "I can't afford to give," or "I'm currently having some financial problems and can't give too much." Plant that seed, and let "... God that giveth the increase," bless you with a harvest (1 Corinthians 3:7).

You can only experience a true increase *after* planting the seeds.

No Seed Planting = No Increase.

No Increase = No Wealthy Place.

❑ SWITCH NINE: PATIENCE.

> **That ye be not slothful, but followers of them who through faith and patience inherit the promises.**
>
> **—Hebrews 6:12**

You don't want to ruin your harvest by trying to grope and grab for it before it's fully matured. There is a rhythm to giving and a rhythm to reaping, and both require patience. That is what God's contention was with Cain. Abel planted in faith; Cain did not. Abel's offering was accepted by God; Cain's was not. When you plant seeds of money into God's work, patience must kick in, or we will grow restless wanting to see results. Some people give up and kill their harvest, trying to extract it before it's ripe.

❑ SWITCH TEN: HARD WORK.

> **Hard workers have plenty of food; playing around brings poverty.**
>
> **—Proverbs 28:19 (NLT)**

> Hard work means prosperity; only fools idle away their time.
>
> —Proverbs 12:11 (NLT)

> If you love sleep, you will end in poverty. Keep your eyes open, and there will be plenty to eat!
>
> —Proverbs 20:13 (NLT)

The Bible says if a man doesn't provide for those of his household, he has denied the faith and is worse than an infidel.

> But if any provide not for his own, and specially for those of his own house, he hath denied the faith, and is worse than an infidel.
>
> —1 Timothy 5:8

Some people die without leaving any inheritance, just bills and debts, and then we preachers get up in the pulpit and say, "He was such a good man." But the Bible says, "A good man leaves an inheritance to his children's children," not thousands of dollars in bills plus an unpaid mortgage. Let your good heart show through hard work.

> A good man leaveth an inheritance to his children's children.
>
> —Proverbs 13:22

❏ SWITCH ELEVEN: DILIGENCE.

> Lazy people want much but get little, but those who work hard will prosper and be satisfied.
>
> —Proverbs 13:4 (NLT)

> "Unless you are faithful in small matters, you won't be faithful in large ones.
>
> —Luke 16:10 (NLT)

Proverbs 24:3-4 gives a three-point plan for diligence: (1) Wisdom, (2) Understanding, (3) Knowledge. That's how I endeavor to run everything in my life. Read it and learn!

> Through wisdom is an house builded; and by understanding it is established:
>
> And by knowledge shall the chambers be filled with all precious and pleasant riches.
>
> —Proverbs 24:3-4

❑ SWITCH TWELVE: RESIST THE DEVIL!

When the devil comes against your finances, resist him with every weapon you have at your disposal. James 4:7-8a says, "Submit yourselves therefore to God. Resist the devil and he will flee from you! Draw nigh to God and he'll draw nigh to you."

WEALTH TRANSFER

Activate these twelve switches and you'll find yourself coming up another level financially. Wealth will begin to chase after you.

WHAT KEEPS PEOPLE OUT

Now let's go through some reminders of what can keep us out of *The Wealthy Place*:

- LACK OF KNOWLEDGE.

> My people are destroyed for lack of knowledge: because thou hast rejected knowledge, I will also reject thee, that thou shalt be no priest to me: seeing thou hast forgotten the law of thy God, I will also forget thy children.

> As they were increased, so they sinned against me: there-
> fore will I change their glory into shame.
>
> —Hosea 4:6-7

As God's children, we have keys to prosperity, but we must pursue practical knowledge.

- **FAITHLESS TALK.**

> Death and life are in the power of the tongue.
>
> —Proverbs 18:21a

Let your words keep you on track. Talk about the wealth God has promised you in Christ. Remind yourself every day of these things. When was the last time you spoke something in faith about yourself financially?

- **UNWILLINGNESS TO PROSPER.**

Some people feel better about themselves in poverty. Isaiah 1:19, "If ye be willing and obedient, ye shall eat the good of the land." Psalm 81:10, "Open thy mouth wide and I will fill it." Some don't open their mouth wide enough for God to fill it! They're satisfied with morsels.

- **UNWILLINGNESS TO START WHERE YOU ARE.**

Some pledge to start tithing only when God gives them more money. If you don't tithe on $80 a week, you won't tithe on $80,000 a week. Put prosperity principles into practice little by little. Nobody goes from A to Z in one step.

- **HAVING NO SPECIFIC FINANCIAL GOALS.**

Some drift through life financially like a ship with no rudder. Wise planning brings success. It isn't going to rain hundred dollar bills on your head, and I can almost guarantee that the sweepstakes man isn't going to knock at your door anytime soon.

- LAZINESS.

God never blesses laziness.

- NOT LISTENING TO GOD'S IDEAS.

God has ideas in store for you — ways to get wealth. Be open to new ideas from Him. His ideas almost always involve risk.

- NOT USING COMMON SENSE.

Walking in the Spirit doesn't mean walking in the weird. God gave us good common sense and expects us to use it. Be shrewd in your business deals.

- SEEKING PERSONAL ADVANCEMENT OVER KINGDOM ADVANCEMENT.

Matthew 6:33: "But seek ye first the Kingdom of God, and his righteousness; and all these things shall be added unto you." If you seek your personal advancement first you may move ahead, but it'll be without God's blessing.

- NOT PAYING YOUR PASTOR OR MINISTER PROPERLY.

As you and your church prosper, your pastor ought to prosper too. Never go a year without giving your pastor a pay raise. I don't care whether he needs it or not.

For two years I didn't take a pay raise at our church. Our attendance leveled off and our income started going down. One of the elders suggested it was because they hadn't given me a raise. I told them I didn't want a raise but they gave me a nice pay raise anyway, and do you know what happened? The church started growing again, and the church income went back up. The man of God is tied to your success.

> Elders who do their work well should be paid well, especially those who work hard at both preaching and teaching.
>
> For the Scripture says, "Do not keep an ox from eating as it treads out the grain." And in another place, "Those who work deserve their pay"!
>
> —1 Timothy 5:17-18 (NLT)

• NOT PLANTING SEEDS.

I have learned that I must plant seeds in ministries, in ministers, and in places where God speaks to me. He has prompted me to give to the church's college kids every so often. I do the same with my Aunt Jane. The Lord spoke to me one time and said I could honor my dad, who died when I was fifteen, by honoring his only living sister. She lives in a little house in Jackson, Michigan. Every so often I'll go to the bank, get a $100 or $50 bill, stick it in an envelope, write her a letter and send it. I tell her, "Here's your hot-dog money!" When I started doing that, something supernatural was unleashed in my life. Different people and ministries sent me checks for thousands of dollars, made out to me personally. They never did that before. I believe it'll happen to you too!

Finally, I'll give you ten simple rules for wealth, plus Scriptures I've compiled to help you pray about your financial future. The rules should look familiar by now, and the prayers will help you soar with God's vision for your finances. You might tear this next page out and stick it on your refrigerator, if it'll help you put the principles into practice.

TEN SIMPLE RULES FOR A LIFE OF WEALTH

1. Put God first in *everything*. Give Him your best. Look to Him as your source and expect Him to give you a harvest.

2. Obey God *at all costs,* even when you don't understand.

3. If you use a credit card, make sure you pay the full balance every month. NEVER incur interest!

4. Wipe out all consumer debt and NEVER AGAIN borrow on anything that depreciates (cars, stereo equipment, furniture, travel, consumer goods).

5. Always pay extra every month on your house payment and NEVER borrow more than you can pay off in seven years or less.

6. Read about and study wealth in God's Word and listen to faith-building cassettes and CDs by people who have beaten debt and are now living in *The Wealthy Place.*

7. Know what you want and *put it in writing*. Read it daily and pray over it regularly. Get a wealth notebook just for your financial dreams and prayer requests.

8. Always, *always* bless the man of God. He has incredible pressures you know nothing about. Bless him whether or not you think he needs it. This includes the pastor, evangelist, district superintendent, and missionary.

9. Determine to NEVER be enslaved by consumer debt again (things that depreciate in value; cars, stereos, furniture, etc.).

10. Open your storehouse accounts (investment accounts) so God can bless you in them. Put AT LEAST 10 percent of your gross income into your storehouses each payday, after bringing your tithes and offerings to God's storehouse.

PRAYER SCRIPTURES FOR YOUR PROSPERITY

Ask of me, and I shall give thee the heathen for thine inheritance, and the uttermost parts of the earth [real estate] for thy possession.

—Psalms 2:8

The earth [real estate] is the LORD'S, and the fulness thereof; the world, and they that dwell therein.

—Psalms 24:1

Blessed are the meek: for they shall inherit the earth [real estate].

—Matthew 5:5

Enlarge the place of thy tent, and let them stretch forth the curtains of thine habitations...for thou shalt break forth on the right hand and on the left.

—Isaiah 54:2a-3a

"But thou shalt remember the LORD thy God: for it is he that giveth thee power to get wealth."

—Deuteronomy 8:18a

Wealth and riches shall be in his house: and his righteousness endureth for ever.

—Psalm 112:3

...and the wealth of the sinner is laid up for the just.

—Proverbs 13:22b

...but thou broughtest us out into a wealthy place.

—Psalm 66:12b

Let the LORD be magnified, which hath pleasure in the prosperity of his servant.

—Psalm 35:27b

...O LORD, I beseech thee, send now prosperity.

—Psalm 118:25b

...believe his [the Lord's] prophets, so shall ye prosper.

—2 Chronicles 20:20c

Beloved, I wish above all things that thou mayest prosper and be in health, even as thy soul prospereth.

—3 John 1:2

Y*ou may need to start thinking bigger,
having a God-sized vision. Whatever the
nugget of truth is that you take with you
from this book, I want it to grow for you.*

CONCLUSION

We've come to the end of this book, but you might want to read it again and again until the principles seep all the way into your spirit. The lessons we've learned are simple, yet profound. Many involve changes you need to make — changes in your life-style, your attitude toward money, your allocation of assets. You may need to get rid of certain things that drag down your finances. You may need to start thinking bigger, having a God-sized vision. Whatever that nugget of truth is that you take with you, I want it to grow for you.

I'd like to conclude with a prayer for you. Agree with me now:

"Father, I ask that You give this reader a deep revelation of Your plan for wealth. Never again will this dear one speak against someone with money, because he or she is going to step up to the concierge level; The Wealthy Place. Help this precious person to get a handle on debt, to make wise investments, to follow the leading of Your Spirit in all financial decisions, and most of all, to put your Kingdom first.

Now I pray, dear reader, that the Lord bless you, prosper you, and give you an unfolding revelation of His deep love for you. I pray that blessings will chase you going home and going to work. I pray that ideas from Heaven will come to your spirit and be transferred to your mind. I pray God will give you a clear plan for the prosperity He's preparing to pour into your life soon. I pray that you will move to the concierge level of radical riches. I pray it, I believe it, I speak it, and I decree it for your life, my friend. In the powerful name of Jesus. Amen!

ABOUT
THE AUTHOR
AND RELATED
MINISTRIES

ABOUT THE AUTHOR

Dr. Dave Williams is pastor of Mount Hope Church and International Outreach Ministries, with world headquarters in Lansing, Michigan. He has served for over 20 years, leading the church in Lansing from 226 to over 4000 today. Dave sends trained ministers into unreached cities to establish disciple-making churches, and, as a result, today has "branch" churches in the United States, Philippines, and in Africa.

Dave is the founder and president of Mount Hope Bible Training Institute, a fully accredited institute for training ministers and lay people for the work of the ministry. He has authored over 55 books including the fifteen-time best seller, *The New Life...The Start of Something Wonderful* (with over 2,000,000 books sold), and more recently, *The Miracle Results of Fasting*, *The Road To Radical Riches*, and *Angels-They Are Watching You!*

The Pacesetter's Path telecast is Dave's weekly television program seen over a syndicated network of secular stations, and nationally over the *Sky Angel* satellite system. He is also seen worldwide on the *TCT* Satellite System, receiving over 1,000 salvation calls to the prayer center weekly. Dave has produced over 125 audio cassette programs including the nationally acclaimed *School of Pacesetting Leadership* which is being used as a training program in churches around the United States, and in Bible Schools in South Africa, South America, Mexico, and the Philippines. He is a popular speaker at conferences, seminars, and conventions.

Along with his wife, Mary Jo, Dave established The Dave and Mary Jo Williams Charitable Mission (Strategic Global Mission), a mission's ministry for providing scholarships to pioneer pastors and grants to inner-city children's ministries.

Dave and Mary Jo own *Sun Prime Equities*, a Florida island condo enterprise.

Dave's articles and reviews have appeared in national magazines such as *Advance*, *The Pentecostal Evangel*, *Ministries Today*, *The Lansing Magazine*, *The Detroit Free Press* and others.

He developed curriculum for *The School of Intercessors* and *The School of Successful Church Planting*. Both are being taught in churches across the United States. Dave, as a private pilot, flies for fun. He is married, has two grown children, and lives in Delta Township, Michigan.

You may write to Pastor Dave Williams:

P.O. Box 80825

Lansing, MI 48908-0825

Please include your special prayer requests when you write, or you may call the Mount Hope Global Prayer Center: (517) 327-PRAY

For a catalog of products, call:

1-517-321-2780 or

1-800-888-7284

or visit us on the web at:

www.mounthopechurch.org

Gilead Healing Center

Gilead
HEALING CENTER

- **The Place Of Another Chance**
- **Training For The Healing Ministry**

- *Prayer*
- *Nutrition*
- *Counseling*
- *Medical*

517-321-2780

We're here for you!
Lansing, Michigan

Other Wealth Building Material by Dave Williams

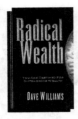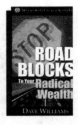

Radical Wealth (5 Audio Tape Set)   *$30.00*

You can break the power of poverty in your life and move into the wealth of God's abundance. Dave Williams shows you the practical, biblical ways to increase and multiplication in your life. Are you ready to jump from "barely getting by" to God's plan for your RADICAL WEALTH? (Cassette Only)

Wealth 101 (5 Audio Set)   *$36.00*

Most people try to increase their income without changing their concepts of wealth. As a result they continue to find themselves struggling to pay the bills, meet the all-too-often "emergencies." They need a revelation from God. This is not just another "prosperity series." This is a divine revelation that can bring you into the place the Psalmist called "The Wealthy Place."
(Available on Cassette & CD)

Road Blocks To Your Wealth (12 Audio Tape Set) *$72.00*

We all yearn to be free of financial pressures. Yet so many of God's precious children are still living in bondage to lack. The scars of yesterday, the programming of the past, the false beliefs, and perhaps a hundred other things hold them back from enjoying God's wonderful promises of prosperity and wealth. Watch out for the Roadblocks to Radical Wealth.

To Order Call: **517-321-2780** **800-888-7284**	*or*	Write: **The Hope Store** **202 South Creyts Road** **Lansing, Michigan 48917-9284**

Please include $4.95 for Shipping and Handling (any size order)

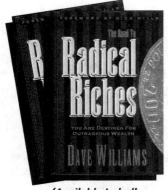

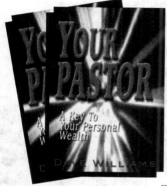

When you face a struggle...
When you need a miracle...

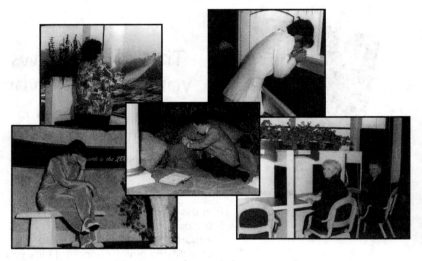

...we'll stand with you in prayer.

GLOBAL PRAYER CENTER

We believe Jesus Christ is the same yesterday, today and forever (Hebrews 13:6).

Our prayer partners will agree with you in prayer for your miracle (Matthew 18:18-19).

Call Anytime (517) 327-PRAY

The Mount Hope Global Prayer Center in Lansing, Michigan

A Dave and Mary Jo Williams Charitable Ministry
P.O. Box 80825 • Lansing • MI 48908-0825

* Training pastors to be successful leaders in God's Kingdom
* Reaching children before the gangs, the cults, and the drugs do

WORDS FROM SCHOLARSHIP RECIPIENTS:

"I do not receive any financial assistance from my local assembly, and this is all the more reason why I am so thankful for your scholarship. It thrills my soul to know that God uses His Church universal to fulfill His plans in the lives of His children."   — C. Rutter

"I stand amazed as I see the hand of God at work through different individuals performing His wonders. Here I am in South Africa thousands of miles away from the States, unknown to you, and yet, I receive a scholarship from you. I thank God, bless His holy name!" — D. Hendricks

Strategic Global Mission helps accelerate world missions, and strengthens local churches by providing scholarships to pioneer pastors and gives grants to targeted inner-city children's ministries. You can provide a much-needed scholarship in your name. You will receive a beautiful certificate with your tax-deductible gift of just $300 or $30 per month. Please write to: Strategic Global Mission, PO Box 80825, Lansing, MI 48908-0825.

OTHER PRODUCTS FROM DECAPOLIS PUBLISHING

FOR YOUR SPIRITUAL GROWTH

Here's the help you need for your spiritual journey. These books will encourage you, and give you guidance as you seek to draw close to Jesus and learn of Him. Prepare yourself for fantastic growth!

RADICAL FASTING
How would you like to achieve your dreams at "break-neck" speed? Radical fasting may be your key!

REGAINING YOUR SPIRITUAL MOMENTUM
Use this remarkable book as your personal street map to regain your spiritual momentum.

THE JEZEBEL SPIRIT
Do you feel controlled? Learn more about what the Bible says about this manipulating principality's influence.

DEVELOPING THE SPIRIT OF A CONQUEROR
Take back what the enemy has stolen from you. Learn how to engage your authority and Develop the Spirit of a Conqueror.

BEAUTY OF HOLINESS
We face the choice — holiness or rebellion. True holiness comes about by working together in cooperation with the Holy Spirit.

ABCs OF SUCCESS & HAPPINESS
God wants to give you every good gift, so it's time to accept the responsibility for your success today!

These and other books available from Dave Williams and:

DECAPOLIS PUBLISHING

FOR YOUR SPIRITUAL GROWTH

Here's the help you need for your spiritual journey. These books will encourage you, and give you guidance as you seek to draw close to Jesus and learn of Him. Prepare yourself for fantastic growth!

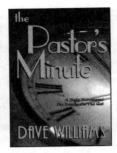

QUESTIONS I HAVE ANSWERED
Get answers to many of the questions you've always wanted to ask a pastor!

THE PASTOR'S MINUTE
A daily devotional for people on the go! Powerful topics will help you grow even when you're in a hurry.

ANGELS: THEY ARE WATCHING YOU!
The Bible tells more than you might think about these powerful beings.

THE WORLD BEYOND
What will Heaven be like? What happens there? Will we see relatives who have gone before us? Who REAL-LY goes to Heaven?

FILLED!
Learn how you can be filled with the mightiest power in the universe. Find out what could be missing from your life.

STRATEGIC GLOBAL MISSION
Read touching stories about God's plan for accelerating the Gospel globally through reaching children and training pastors.

These and other books available from Dave Williams and:

DECAPOLIS PUBLISHING

FOR YOUR SPIRITUAL GROWTH

Here's the help you need for your spiritual journey. These books will encourage you, and give you guidance as you seek to draw close to Jesus and learn of Him. Prepare yourself for fantastic growth!

HOW TO BE A HIGH PERFORMANCE BELIEVER
Pour in the nine spiritual additives for real power in your Christian life.

SECRET OF POWER WITH GOD
Tap into the real power with God; the power of prayer. It will change your life!

THE NEW LIFE . . .
You can get off to a great start on your exciting life with Jesus! Prepare for something wonderful.

MIRACLE RESULTS OF FASTING
You can receive MIRACLE benefits, spiritually and physically, with this practical Christian discipline.

WHAT TO DO IF YOU MISS THE RAPTURE
If you miss the Rapture, there may still be hope, but you need to follow these clear survival tactics.

THE AIDS PLAGUE
Is there hope? Yes, but only Jesus can bring a total and lasting cure to AIDS.

These and other books available from Dave Williams and:

DECAPOLIS PUBLISHING

FOR YOUR SPIRITUAL GROWTH

Here's the help you need for your spiritual journey. These books will encourage you, and give you guidance as you seek to draw close to Jesus and learn of Him. Prepare yourself for fantastic growth!

THE ART OF PACESETTING LEADERSHIP
You can become a successful leader with this proven leadership development course.

GIFTS THAT SHAPE YOUR LIFE
Learn which ministry best fits you, and discover your God-given personality gifts, as well as the gifts of others.

GROWING UP IN OUR FATHER'S FAMILY
You can have a family relationship with your heavenly father. Learn how God cares for you.

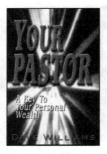

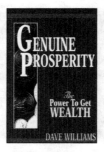

SUPERNATURAL SOULWINNING
How will we reach our family, friends, and neighbors in this short time before Christ's return?

YOUR PASTOR: A KEY TO YOUR PERSONAL WEALTH
By honoring your pastor you can actually be setting yourself up for a financial blessing from God!

GENUINE PROSPERITY
Learn what it means to be truly prosperous! God gives us the power to get wealth!

These and other books available from Dave Williams and:

DECAPOLIS PUBLISHING

FOR YOUR SPIRITUAL GROWTH

Here's the help you need for your spiritual journey. These books will encourage you, and give you guidance as you seek to draw close to Jesus and learn of Him. Prepare yourself for fantastic growth!

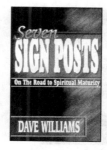

SOMEBODY OUT THERE NEEDS YOU
Along with the gift of salvation comes the great privilege of spreading the Gospel of Jesus Christ.

SEVEN SIGNPOSTS ON THE ROAD TO SPIRITUAL MATURITY
Examine your life to see where you are on the road to spiritual maturity.

THE PASTOR'S PAY
How much is your pastor worth? Who should set his pay? Discover the scriptural guidelines for paying your pastor.

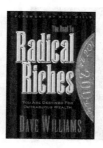

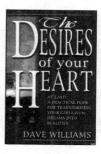

DECEPTION, DELUSION & DESTRUCTION
Recognize spiritual deception and unmask spiritual blindness.

THE ROAD TO RADICAL RICHES
Are you ready to jump from "barely getting by" to God's plan for putting you on the road to Radical Riches?

THE DESIRES OF YOUR HEART
Yes, Jesus wants to give you the desires of your heart, and make them realities.

These and other books available from Dave Williams and:

DECAPOLIS PUBLISHING

FOR YOUR SUCCESSFUL LIFE

These video cassettes will give you successful principles to apply to your whole life. Each a different topic, and each a fantastic teaching of how living by God's Word can give you total success!

THE PRESENCE OF GOD
Find out how you can have a more dynamic relationship with the Holy Spirit.

FILLED WITH THE HOLY SPIRIT
You can rejoice and share with others in this wonderful experience of God.

GIFTS THAT CHANGE YOUR WORLD
Learn which ministry best fits you, and discover your God-given personality gifts, as well as the gifts of others.

 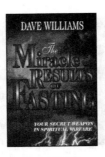 

THE SCHOOL OF PACESETTING LEADERSHIP
Leaders are made, not born. You can become a successful leader with this proven leadership development course.

MIRACLE RESULTS OF FASTING
Fasting is your secret weapon in spiritual warfare. Learn how you'll benefit spiritually and physically! Six video messages.

A SPECIAL LADY
If you feel used and abused, this video will show you how you really are in the eyes of Jesus. You are special!

These and other videos available from Dave Williams and:

DECAPOLIS PUBLISHING

FOR YOUR SUCCESSFUL LIFE

These video cassettes will give you successful principles to apply to your whole life. Each a different topic, and each a fantastic teaching of how living by God's Word can give you total success!

HOW TO BE A HIGH PERFORMANCE BELIEVER
Pour in the nine spiritual additives for real power in your Christian life.

THE UGLY WORMS OF JUDGMENT
Recognizing the decay of judgment in your life is your first step back into God's fullness.

WHAT TO DO WHEN YOU FEEL WEAK AND DEFEATED
Learn about God's plan to bring you out of defeat and into His principles of victory!

WHY SOME ARE NOT HEALED
Discover the obstacles that hold people back from receiving their miracle and how God can help them receive the very best!

BREAKING THE POWER OF POVERTY
The principality of mammon will try to keep you in poverty. Put God FIRST and watch Him bring you into a wealthy place.

HERBS FOR HEALTH
A look at the concerns and fears of modern medicine. Learn the correct ways to open the doors to your healing.

These and other videos available from Dave Williams and:

DECAPOLIS PUBLISHING

RUNNING YOUR RACE

These simple but powerful audio cassette singles will help give you the edge you need. Run your race to win!

LONELY IN THE MIDST OF A CROWD
Loneliness is a devastating disease. Learn how to trust and count on others to help.

HERBS FOR HEALTH
A look at the concerns and fears of modern medicine. Learn the correct ways to open the doors to your healing.

HOW TO GET ANYTHING YOU WANT
You can learn the way to get anything you want from God!

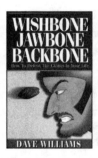

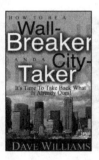

WISHBONE, JAWBONE, BACKBONE
Learn about King David, and how his three "bones" for success can help you in your life quest.

FATAL ENTICEMENTS
Learn how you can avoid the vice-like grip of sin and it's fatal enticements that hold people captive.

HOW TO BE A WALL BREAKER AND A CITY TAKER
You can be a powerful force for advancing the Kingdom of Jesus Christ!

These and other audio tapes available from Dave Williams and:

DECAPOLIS PUBLISHING

EXPANDING YOUR FAITH

These exciting audio teaching series will help you to grow and mature in your walk with Christ. Get ready for amazing new adventures in faith!

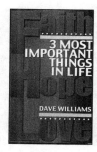

THE BLESSING
Explore the many ways that God can use you to bless others, and how He can correct the missed blessing.

SIN'S GRIP
Learn how you can avoid the vice-like grip of sin and its fatal enticements that hold people captive.

FAITH, HOPE, & LOVE
Listen and let these three "most important things in life" change you.

**PSALM 91
THE PROMISE OF
PROTECTION**
Everyone is looking for protection in these perilous times. God promises protection for those who rest in Him.

**DEVELOPING
THE SPIRIT OF A
CONQUEROR**
You can be a conqueror through Christ! Also, find out how to keep those things that you have conquered.

WHY DO SOME SUFFER
Find out why some people seem to have suffering in their lives, and how to avoid it in your life.

*These and other audio tapes
available from Dave Williams and:*

**DECAPOLIS
PUBLISHING**

EXPANDING YOUR FAITH

These exciting audio teaching series will help you to grow and mature in your walk with Christ. Get ready for amazing new adventures in faith!

ABCs OF SUCCESS AND HAPPINESS
Learn how to go after God's promises for your life. Happiness and success can be yours today!

FORGIVENESS
The miracle remedy for many of life's problems is found in this basic key for living.

UNTANGLING YOUR TROUBLES
You can be a "trouble untangler" with the help of Jesus!

HOW TO BE A HIGH PER-FORMANCE BELIEVER
Put in the nine spiritual additives to help run your race and get the prize!

BEING A DISCIPLE AND MAKING DISCIPLES
You can learn to be a "disciple maker" to almost anyone.

HOW TO HELP YOUR PAS-TOR & CHURCH SUCCEED
You can be an integral part of your church's & pastor's success.

These and other audio tapes available from Dave Williams and:

DECAPOLIS PUBLISHING